Sexuality

HEALTH FACTS

Lucas Stang

and

Kathleen R. Miner, PhD, MPH, CHES

ETR ASSOCIATES

Santa Cruz, California

1994

 iing and Research) is a nonprofit organization
well-being and cultural diversity of individuals,
families, schools and communities. The publishing program of ETR Associates provides books and materials that empower young people and adults with the skills to make positive health choices. We invite health professionals to learn more about our high-quality publishing, training and research programs by contacting us at P.O. Box 1830, Santa Cruz, CA 95061-1830, 1-800-321-4407.

Published by ETR Associates, P.O. Box 1830,
Santa Cruz, California 95061-1830

Printed in the United States of America
Designed by Ann Smiley
10 9 8 7 6 5 4 3
Title No. H307

Library of Congress Cataloging-in-Publication Data

Stang, Lucas.
    Sexuality : health facts / Lucas Stang, Kathleen R.
Miner.
        p. cm.
    Includes bibliographical references.
    ISBN 1-56071-187-6
    1. Sex instruction—United States. I. Miner, Kathleen
Rae, 1946–   . II. Title.
HQ57.5.A3S73   1994
613.9'07—dc20   93-41374

Contents

Sexuality

Editor's Preface

Everyone agrees that children and youth need to learn skills for establishing good health habits. Most people also agree that the earlier health education starts, the better its success.

The books in the *Health Facts* series were written to provide the background information educators need as they teach young people about health. The information is provided in a way that makes it easy for educators to familiarize themselves quickly with the most important facts about a health topic.

Rather than providing indepth information in each content area, the books offer guidance to the balance of emphasis. They help educators approach health topics with confidence and focus health content as they teach.

Titles in the Series

Each volume in the series contains information about a different content area. The following books comprise the series:

- *Abstinence*
- *Disease*
- *Drugs*
- *Environmental and Community Health*
- *Fitness*
- *HIV*
- *Injury Prevention*
- *Nutrition and Body Image*
- *Self-Esteem and Mental Health*
- *Sexuality*
- *STD*
- *Tobacco*
- *Violence*

Contributors

These books were written by the following talented and knowledgeable professionals in collaboration with ETR Associates' staff.

Nora Krantzler, PhD, MPH, is a freelance writer and researcher who specializes in issues related to health. She has a doctorate in medical anthropology and a master's in epidemiology. Her work has been presented in professional journals, at meetings of professional societies, in government reports and policy manuals, and in other books. Topics have included nutrition issues, child abuse and neglect, and medical practice.

Kathleen R. Miner, PhD, MPH, CHES, is associate professor and coordinator of health promotion and education in the Division of Behavioral Science and Health Education at Emory University School of Public Health. She has traveled internationally as a health educator and is the author of many articles about education and health. A former high school health and biology teacher, she has been a key contributor in designing these books to be useful to teachers.

Lucas Stang has a background in biology and health, with graduate work in science communication. He has been writing health materials for ten years. He recently served as wellness coordinator for the International School in Manila, Philippines, where he developed a kindergarten through grade 12 health curriculum and taught high school health. He has also taught human sexuality at the junior college level.

Netha L. Thacker is project editor for the *Health Facts* series. She has been involved in the development of health education materials for more than five years, on topics including puberty, adolescent sexuality, and prevention of HIV and other sexually transmitted disease. She has an extensive background in journalism, writing and editing and has been the editor of statewide newsletters for both the California AIDS Clearinghouse and the Tobacco Education Clearinghouse of California.

Acknowledgments

We would like to thank the following people, who provided reviews and content expertise.

John T. Boothby, PhD, is an associate professor at San Jose State University in San Jose, California, where he teaches microbiology and immunology.

Rama Khalsa, PhD, is a clinical psychologist and the director of the Santa Cruz County Department of Mental Health in Santa Cruz, California.

Wendy J. Schiff, MS, is a technical writing specialist in health and nutrition and teaches health at St. Louis Community College in St. Louis, Missouri.

We would also like to thank Mary Nelson, publisher of ETR Associates, for the concept idea, Kathleen Middleton, editor-in-chief of ETR Associates, for her review and conceptualization, and Susan Bagby and Jill Schettler for their help in editing.

Introduction

"Love makes the world go around," goes the old
adage, but the truth is that sex ensures that the
species continues so that it can tangle with emotional concepts like love. Without love the world
would be a pretty bleak place, but without sex,
we'd die out in a generation.

—Carol Cassell

For most of human history, people did not connect reproduction with sexual intercourse. After all, a woman's belly did not
begin to swell until many months after the act, and she did
not give birth until nine months later. Even when the relationship between sexual intercourse and reproduction was well
established, people ascribed much of the reproductive process
to mystery and magic.

It was not until the twentieth century that people began to
understand the mechanisms of conception and contraception,
the processes of pregnancy and prenatal development, and the
role of genes and chromosomes. Parallel with these advances

in the scientific understanding of the human reproductive process, scientists began to take an interest in studying human sexuality independent of its reproductive role.

Researchers such as Freud, Kinsey, and Masters and Johnson challenged traditional views of what it means to be reproductive and what it means to be sexual. Although some of their procedures and conclusions were and are controversial, their work has given us much to think about.

This work lessened the taboos associated with candid conversations about human sexual matters. Human sexuality and the role it plays in defining personal identity, intimacy and love are now topics of discussion not only for intimate couples, but also between doctor and patient, minister and parishioner, teacher and student, and parent and child.

During the twentieth century, American society has moved through a rapid succession of different phases of sexuality. These phases include:

- the residue of the Victorian era, with high collars and denial of sexual passion
- the post–World War I era, with flappers, the Charleston and the birth control crusades of Margaret Sanger
- the Depression years, with their enormous poverty, booming contraceptive business, and the beginning of tax-supported birth control clinics
- the World War II years, with the roots of feminism in Rosie the Riveter and women in the armed services
- the cold war decades, with rock and roll, middle-class suburban lifestyles and unprecedented contraceptive freedom
- the 1970s, with the rise in single-parent households, herpes and feminism
- the 1980s, with sexual liberalism, teenage pregnancy and cohabitation without marriage
- the 1990s, with the HIV/AIDS epidemic, focus on condoms, acknowledgment of sexual abuse and date rape, and sexual politics.

The twentieth century has seen great change in the American sexual ethic. The American public has yet to come to terms with what all this change means.

With so many changes in such a short time, what will the next decades bring? Regardless of the answer to this question, the next generation of human beings must understand the need to protect themselves from sexual dangers. They need an awareness of the complexities of reproduction and love that they will inevitably face. In spite of the anxiety such education may cause the adults in charge, America's youth need appropriate, straightforward sexuality education in their homes, schools and communities.

Sexuality: Health Facts provides teachers with the basics of the anatomy and physiology of male and female reproductive systems. The book presents a brief overview of pregnancy and birth, puberty and adolescence, and contraceptives. It also discusses a range of adolescent sexual behaviors and the differences between love and sex.

The Role of Education

The research conducted during the past thirty years has offered greater insight into the causes of chronic disease, injury and violence. This research indicates that these conditions are primarily caused by human behavior. What people do or do not do places them at risk of acquiring chronic diseases or experiencing serious injuries.

The behavioral components associated with the modern pattern of disease and injury create the potential for preventing most of these health problems by changing behavior. Comprehensive health promotion and education programs provide the foundation for modern disease prevention.

Ideally, the health promotion and education process begins early. Early education provides the opportunity to reach children and youth before they begin to adopt the behaviors associated with chronic disease, sexually transmitted disease, drug use, injury and mental illness. Through a systematic review of health promotion and disease prevention, educators can help children and youth enhance their health while helping them avoid illness and injury.

The *Health Facts* Series

Sexuality: Health Facts is part of a series designed to provide clear, concise content and to be complementary to curricula published by ETR Associates and other health education curricula. Other volumes in this series that relate to sexuality include *Abstinence, Disease, Self-Esteem and Mental Health, STD* and *HIV.*

Classroom teachers, counselors, school nurses and others are often called upon to become instant health educators. They may be asked to answer questions, present information and lead discussions on health topics in which they feel unprepared.

The *Health Facts* series is designed to be a handy reference for individuals who would like additional background information on particular health topics. The emphasis is on topics and examples that are relevant to youth of middle and high school age. By design, the presentation of each of the topics is brief. References and resource listings direct the reader to additional relevant information. All of the volumes in this series offer a user-friendly format that is easy to read and factual.

The volumes discuss health and disease in straightforward language. Educators may want to review each volume for its appropriateness for their school and community before assigning the books for student use.

This book and the rest of the series can serve as useful additions to classroom, school or library collections. Health care professionals may choose individual volumes or the entire series as a convenient reference for patient education programs or as reading material in office waiting rooms. Individuals may find the series useful as a home reference as well.

Learning About Sexuality

MYTH: Sexuality begins during puberty.

Fact: Sexuality is an entire dimension of human development that begins before birth and extends throughout life.

The term *sexuality* refers to the totality of being a person. Human beings are sexual when they participate in sexual acts, but they are sexual at all other times as well.

A comprehensive study of sexuality rests on a firm foundation of biological understanding. But the various dimensions of sexuality are overlapping, not discrete. It is impossible to talk about human reproduction, for example, without discussing its cultural, psychosocial or ethical considerations. All aspects of sexuality are interconnected.

What Is Sexuality?

Sexuality includes all aspects of being male or female. It has at least four dimensions:

- biological
- psychosocial
- ethical
- cultural

■ The **biological** dimension of sexuality involves:

- physical appearance, including the development of physical sexual characteristics
- sexual desire and response to sexual stimulation
- the ability to reproduce or to control fertility
- general growth and development

Although humans cannot reproduce until puberty, sexual functioning begins at birth and lasts a lifetime.

■ The **psychosocial** dimension of sexuality refers to people's attitudes about themselves and others. These attitudes are shaped by experience, through which people learn how to express emotions and behave as sexual beings. This learning involves not only what people do, but how and why they do it. Regardless of whether individuals' experiences are positive or negative, their learned responses to their experience become inseparable from their sexuality.

■ The **ethical** dimension is concerned with moral values that affect sexuality. Morals are structured by questions people ask about behavior and their decisions about what is right and wrong, based on religious beliefs, family values or some other ethical system.

■ The **cultural** dimension is the sum of all the cultural influences, both historical and contemporary, that affect thought and actions. Many beliefs about sexuality are relative to time, place and circumstance. Sexual customs, gender roles and laws regulating sexual practices are all functions of culture. Cultural influences include the media, social institutions and interpersonal relationships.

Educating About Sexuality

Many people have incorrect expectations of sexuality education programs. Some believe that sexuality education encourages sexual behavior or that students become more permissive or liberal. Others believe that sexuality education programs will stop teenage pregnancies, reduce sexual activity or eliminate sexually transmitted disease.

None of these expectations is realistic. However, good sexuality education programs, which are well planned and well carried out, involve properly trained personnel, and are properly evaluated, do provide the following benefits:

- put sexuality in its proper perspective, as one part of total personality
- combat distorted images of sexuality common in the media
- provide factual information that helps reduce misconceptions
- provide insight and understanding to aid responsible decision making

Reasons for Sexuality Education

Bruess and Laing (1989) offer the following three reasons for sexuality education.

1. Sexual adjustment is part of total personality adjustment. Sexuality education can put sexuality in its proper perspective. Although sexuality is but one part of total personality, it is an important part.

   People need to understand their sexual nature and needs as well as changing sexual roles. It is important to keep in mind that human sexuality is part of human personality.

2. People receive a distorted view of life through the mass media. It is common to see sexual themes on television, in movies and in magazines and books. Sexuality education can place these aspects of life in their true perspective.

   Promiscuity, broken marriages, illicit love affairs and prostitution do happen in real life, but they are not as common as the media seem to indicate. Emphasis should be on the relationship of sexuality to positive human relationships and personal feelings. Sexuality education programs can provide this perspective.

3. Young people receive much false information from peers and other sources. In fact, peers are the primary source of sexuality information for most young people today. Sexuality education can give factual information that will help reduce many misconceptions. Learners can then gain insight and understanding that will aid responsible decision making.

1-Minute Facts

- Sexuality has at least four dimensions: biological, psycho-social, ethical and cultural.

- Sexuality education can be very effective if it is based on a high-quality program and realistic expectations.

Female Sexual Anatomy and Physiology

Myth: Just as men continually make sperm, women continually make egg cells.

Fact: Women are born with all the egg cells they will ever have, somewhere between a quarter and half a million. About 400 of these eggs will mature and be ovulated during a woman's reproductive lifetime.

The External Organs

Most of a woman's sexual organs are safely protected within the body. The exterior organs are as follows:

- mons pubis
- labia majora
- labia minora
- clitoris
- vaginal opening
- urethral opening

They are collectively called the *vulva*.

Although the female breasts are not truly reproductive organs, they serve an important reproductive function in providing milk for a newborn infant.

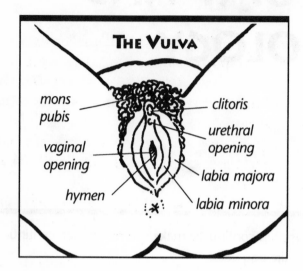

THE VULVA

mons pubis

vaginal opening

hymen

clitoris

urethral opening

labia majora

labia minora

The external female sexual organs are collectively called the vulva.

■ The **mons pubis** consists of fatty tissue under the skin that covers the point called the *pubic symphysis* where the pelvic bones come together. In adult women, the mons is covered by pubic hair. Also called the *mons veneris* ("mound of Venus" or "mountain of love"), this is the most visible portion of the female genitals.

The mons pubis has two functions. It acts as a cushion to protect the underlying bone. Also, since the area is filled with nerves, stimulation of the mons can produce sexual arousal.

■ The **labia majora,** or *outer lips,* are two folds of skin that begin just above the *clitoris* and end just above the anus, where they merge with other body skin. Pubic hair grows on the lips' dark outer surfaces at puberty. The folds are embedded with sweat glands, oil glands and nerve endings.

Sexuality

Generally, the labia majora are closed along the midline, but during sexual arousal they flatten to expose the inner lips and the vaginal opening. The labia majora protect the vaginal and *urethral* (urinary) openings. They are also a source of sexual sensations.

■ The **labia minora,** or *inner lips,* are two smaller, hairless folds of skin lying within the outer lips. They meet just above the clitoris and form another fold of skin called the *clitoral hood,* sometimes referred to as the female foreskin. These structures have a core of spongy tissue and a rich assortment of blood vessels and nerves. The lips are very sensitive, and during sexual arousal, they swell with blood and turn a deep red color.

They serve as a mechanical barrier that protects the vaginal and urethral openings and as a source of sexual sensations.

Bartholin's glands are two pea-sized glands located within the labia minora. Each has a small *duct* or tube that opens onto the labia on either side of the vaginal opening.

At one time, the glands were thought to be important to vaginal lubrication. However, the few drops of liquid the glands produce during sexual arousal have no role in vaginal lubrication. They may simply moisten the labia.

■ The **clitoris,** located just below the juncture of the inner lips, is a highly sensitive organ similar to the male penis, but without reproductive or urinary functions. It is composed of three parts: *glans, shaft* and *cura.*

The glans projects beyond the clitoral hood and looks like a small, shiny button. The shaft, hidden by the hood, contains two masses of spongy, erectile tissue that fill with blood and swell during sexual arousal. Internally, the shaft branches to form the cura, an inverted "V" that extends into the pelvis.

The only known clitoral function is sexual pleasure.

- The **vaginal opening,** which is technically called the *vaginal introitus*, is visible only when the labia are parted. It is the larger opening located between the entry to the urethra and the anus. Its shape depends to a certain extent on the shape of the hymen. The opening is surrounded by rings of muscles and embedded with nerve fibers and blood vessels. It allows access to the vagina.

  The *hymen* is a thin tissue membrane found only in human females. It can surround, stretch across or cover the vaginal opening. The hymen is not a solid structure; it contains irregular openings to allow menstrual flow and other secretions to leave the body. This membrane has no known physiological function.

  Although most females do have a hymen, some girls are born without one. On rare occasions, a girl is born with a tough, fibrous hymen with no opening. This condition, called an *imperforate hymen*, is usually diagnosed when menstruation begins and the fluid accumulates inside the vagina. A simple surgical procedure can correct the problem with no aftereffects.

- The **urethral opening** is the opening of the *urethra*, the pathway through which urine leaves the body.

- All mammals have **breasts,** but they are particularly well developed in the human female. The breast is composed of four structures:
  - **Mammary glands:** Each breast contains 15 to 25 milk sacs surrounded by fibrous and fatty tissues.
  - **Mammary ducts:** Each gland has a tube, or duct, that connects it to the nipple. Milk is transported through these ducts.
  - **Areola:** This darkened circular area around each nipple contains oil-producing glands, which keep the area from drying out during breast feeding.
  - **Nipple:** This is the tip of the breast into which the milk ducts open. The nipple is richly supplied with nerve

fibers, which make it sensitive. The nipple also has muscles that cause it to become erect during sexual arousal or in response to cold.

Breasts vary in shape and size among women. They can change with age, weight, pregnancy and other factors. There is no correlation between breast size and a woman's level of sexual interest or her ability to breastfeed.

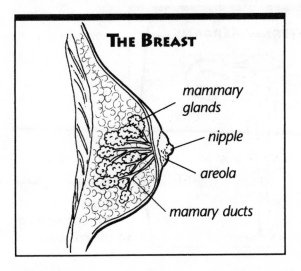

THE BREAST

mammary glands

nipple

areola

mamary ducts

The female breast has four structures.

BREAST EXAMS ARE IMPORTANT

Breast tissue is susceptible to a variety of diseases. Some are harmless; some are very serious. That's why it is important for women to examine their own breasts monthly. The American Cancer Society can provide information about breast self-examination, as can a doctor or local health clinic.

HEALTH FACTS

The Internal Organs

A woman's major reproductive organs are located inside the body cavity. They include:

- vagina
- uterus
- fallopian tubes
- ovaries

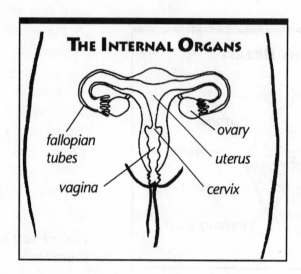

THE INTERNAL ORGANS

fallopian tubes

ovary

uterus

vagina

cervix

The major female reproductive organs are located inside the body.

■ The **vagina,** or *birth canal,* is a flattened tube about three or four inches (8–10 cm) in length that extends from the tip of the uterus to the external opening in the vulva. The organ is muscular and very elastic.

Generally, the tube is closed, but it can expand in both length and width during sexual arousal and childbirth. The vagina will adjust in size to accommodate a finger, a tampon, a penis or a baby. The changes in vaginal size are caused by altered blood flow to the area.

The blood also causes droplets of colorless liquid to ooze through the furrowed vaginal walls in a process similar to sweating. The shiny, slippery lubricant reduces friction as it coats the vagina, making intercourse or childbirth easier.

Sexuality

The upper two-thirds of the vagina has very few nerve endings, making it very insensitive, which helps make childbirth less painful. The portion of the organ near the vaginal opening is sensitive to erotic stimulation.

The vagina is the receptive organ of sexual intercourse in females, and the organ through which the baby is delivered at birth. For some women, it is an important source of sexual pleasure.

■ **The uterus,** sometimes called the *womb*, is an incredibly strong, hollow muscle. In nonpregnant women, the organ is about the size of a fist (approximately three inches or 7.5 cm) and is shaped like an upside-down pear. In the body, it is tilted slightly forward. During pregnancy, the uterus grows to about 12 inches (30.5 cm); it shrinks again after childbirth. The uterus is held in the pelvic cavity by a series of ligaments that allow it to shift and contract. The uterus is composed of three layers:

- The **endometrium,** the innermost layer, is richly supplied with blood vessels. This layer changes during the menstrual cycle, first building up to prepare for a possible pregnancy, then partly sloughing off if pregnancy does not occur. Most of the menstrual flow is the breakdown products of the endometrium.
- The **myometrium** is the thick middle layer composed of very strong, elastic muscles that create the contractions of labor and orgasm.
- The **perimetrium** is the organ's outer covering tissue.

The bottom part, or *neck*, of the uterus dips into the vagina. This portion is known as the *cervix*. It has no surface nerve endings and plays no role in sexual pleasure. In a woman who has never been pregnant, the cervix looks like a shiny, round button with a central hole that allows sperm into the uterus and menstrual flow out. This opening, called the *os*, is about the diameter of a pencil lead; the os can stretch, however, during childbirth to approximately eight inches (10 cm).

The cervix contains many secretory glands that produce *cervical mucus*. The consistency of the mucus changes in response to hormones throughout the menstrual cycle. At ovulation, the mucus is clear and slippery, making it easy for sperm to enter; at other times it is thick and dry, blocking the entrance to the uterus.

The uterus, through its response to hormones, facilitates fertilization, provides a safe and nourishing cavity in which the embryo can develop, and contracts to push the baby out of the body at childbirth.

■ The **fallopian tubes** are threadlike tubes named for the sixteenth century Italian anatomist Gabriello Fallopius, who discovered them. The two tubes are extremely thin—about the width of two human hairs—and extend about four inches into the abdominal cavity from either side of the uterus. Also known as the *oviducts*, they connect the uterus and the ovaries.

The tubes are slightly wider at the ovarian end and fringed with fingerlike projections called *fimbriae*, which wave gently in the surrounding fluid, causing them to stroke the ovary. When an egg leaves the ovary, it is swept into the tube by the fimbriae to begin its journey toward the uterus.

The inside of each fallopian tube is furrowed and lined with tiny hair-like structures called *cilia*. The cilia and contractions of the tube itself move the egg, which is unable to swim as sperm do, along the passageway.

The fallopian tubes act as a passageway for the egg between the ovary and the uterus. They also are the fertilization site for egg and sperm.

The male sperm usually joins the egg in the upper third of the tube, and then the fertilized egg continues to the uterus. However, some conditions, particularly sexually transmitted disease (STD), can cause the narrow tubes to become blocked by scar tissue.

If the tubes are completely closed, the woman is *sterile* because the egg and sperm cannot meet. Other problems can occur when the tube is partially blocked, including *ectopic* or *tubal* pregnancy. In ectopic pregnancy, the fertilized egg implants outside the uterus. Tubal pregnancy occurs when the fertilized egg cannot pass through a partially blocked tube to the uterus.

The tubes are also the most common site of female sterilization, a surgical procedure in which the oviducts are plugged, tied or cut to prevent fertilization. This procedure is called *tubal ligation.*

■ The **ovaries,** two sacs of eggs that lie on either side of the uterus, are the female *gonads.* Each ovary is roughly the size and shape of an almond, about one-and-a-half inches (3 cm) long, held in place by a string of muscle, or *ligament.*

Females are born with all the eggs they will ever have. The ovaries contain an estimated 400,000 immature eggs at birth. Each egg is surrounded by a thin protective capsule called a *follicle.*

Beginning at puberty, one or more of the follicles and its egg matures each menstrual cycle. When the maturation process is complete, the follicle moves to the outer edge of the ovary, ruptures and releases its egg. During a woman's reproductive lifetime, between 400 and 500 eggs will be released.

In addition to maturing and releasing eggs, the ovaries produce the hormones *estrogen* and *progesterone.*

MENSTRUATION IS HEALTHY

Menstruation is not an illness. Menstruating women can swim, exercise, have intercourse, work—whatever is normal for them. Menstruation is healthy. It is not a "curse," but a normal biological function.

HEALTH FACTS

The Menstrual Cycle

Menstruation is a normal part of the female life cycle. Each month, the lining of a nonpregnant woman's uterus is prepared for the possible reception, implantation and support of a fertilized egg. Most of the time, pregnancy does not occur, so the lining breaks up and is shed during the menstrual period, also known as *menses* or *menstruation.*

The cycle begins at puberty, which happens somewhere between age 8 and 16 for most girls. The average age for girls to start menstruating is between 12 and 13. The first cycle is called *menarche.* The cycle repeats during a woman's reproductive years (except during pregnancy) until it stops between the ages of 45 and 55. At the end of her last menstrual cycle, a woman is said to have reached *menopause.*

Cycle length varies from 21 to 40 days. The cycle length can be affected by changes in temperature, altitude, stress levels and other factors. On average, a cycle lasts for one lunar month, or 28 days. It is measured from the first day of menstrual bleeding to the day before the next onset of menstrual bleeding.

The cycle is controlled by the interplay between the brain and the ovaries. The hypothalamus and pituitary glands in the brain secrete hormones that turn on hormone production in the ovaries. The ovarian hormones trigger release of a mature egg and cause changes in the uterus.

Menstrual Phases

The process can be divided into four overlapping phases. Each phase is triggered by changing levels of four hormones:
- follicle stimulating hormone (FSH)
- luteinizing hormone (LH)
- estrogen
- progesterone

These hormones cause changes in the structure and function of the ovary, as well as in the endometrial lining of the uterus. Relating these changes and phases to days in an average cycle gives a visual picture. (See chart.)

■ **Phase 1: Menses** is the time of bleeding, a menstrual period, which lasts about three to seven days. About a quarter cup of fluid is released through the vagina during the entire period. The fluid consists of blood and tissue from the endometrium, and mucus and dead cells from the vagina and cervix.

During the flow, the pituitary gland is secreting high amounts of FSH and a little LH, which stimulates a new set of ovarian follicles to begin to mature. Estrogen and progesterone are at their lowest levels during the menses phase.

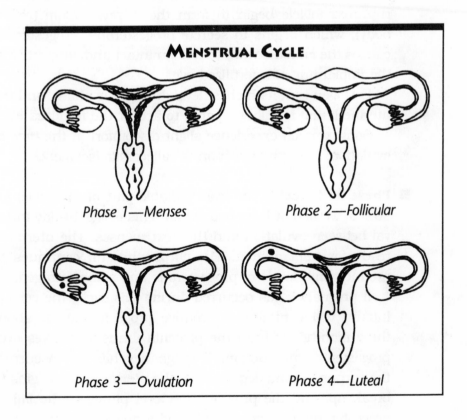

MENSTRUAL CYCLE

Phase 1—Menses

Phase 2—Follicular

Phase 3—Ovulation

Phase 4—Luteal

■ **Phase 2:** The **follicular** phase begins when the menstrual period stops. It lasts on average 12 days, but can vary significantly among women and in the same woman from cycle to cycle. High FSH continues to stimulate the follicle to grow. At a certain level, FSH production ceases. LH increases as the level of FSH begins to fall, which causes the follicle to move toward the outer edge of the ovary. The follicle itself secretes estrogen, which causes the endometrium of the uterus to thicken.

■ **Phase 3:** During **ovulation,** which is at the midpoint of the cycle, LH level reaches its peak, causing the follicle to rupture and release its mature egg. Ovulation is the most fertile time during the cycle.

The follicle remains in the ovary, and at this time assumes a new name and a new function. Cells in the ruptured follicle begin to form the *corpus luteum* (yellow body), which begins to secrete progesterone. Progesterone causes the endometrium to remain intact and supportive of the implanting of a fertilized egg.

Estrogen is at its highest level during this phase, and the uterine lining is fully prepared to accept the fertilized egg.

Some women experience slight discomfort at the time of ovulation. This phenomenon is called *mittelschmerz.*

■ **Phase 4: Luteal** is the least variable part of the cycle; for 90% of women, it lasts two weeks. This is the 14-day interval between ovulation and the next menses. The uterus is ready for implantation. The corpus luteum continues to produce high levels of progesterone and some estrogen.

If pregnancy has occurred during this cycle, the corpus luteum will continue to produce progesterone for about three months, or until the placenta forms and takes over progesterone production. If pregnancy has not occurred, the corpus luteum degenerates, the uterine lining begins to break up, and the progesterone level plunges. The fall in progesterone triggers menses, and a new cycle begins.

Menstrual Problems

Menstruation is a normal and healthy process. However, some women may sometimes have problems. Possible problems include:

- dysmenorrhea
- amenorrhea
- premenstrual syndrome (PMS)
- toxic shock syndrome (TSS)

■ **Dysmenorrhea,** or painful periods, is the most common menstrual problem. Many women will sometimes experience some discomfort, which may include cramping, headache, backache, nausea or a bloated feeling. Although for most women the discomfort is minor, in others the symptoms may be severe enough to interfere with work or school and can last for several days.

There are a variety of ways to relieve dysmenorrhea symptoms, but not all methods work for all women. Exercise and keeping in good physical shape can help. The oldest and simplest drug is aspirin. Ibuprofen drugs such as Advil, Motrin, Nuprin and others can be very effective against menstrual pain. A variety of prescription preparations can also provide relief.

■ **Amenorrhea** is the absence of menstrual periods. If menstruation has not occurred by age 18, the condition is called *primary amenorrhea*. If at least one menstrual period has occurred, it is called *secondary amenorrhea*. It can be caused by pregnancy, tumors, defects in the reproductive system, or emotional factors.

Menstruation depends on body weight or, more specifically, on the ratio of fat to muscle tissue. Women who exercise so much that they have very little body fat—ballet dancers or long-distance runners, for example—often experience secondary amenorrhea. Women with the eating disorder anorexia nervosa do not menstruate for the same reason. The condition can usually be reversed with reduced exercise or better nutrition, but some women have permanent problems.

■ **Premenstrual syndrome (PMS)** is difficult to describe because there is no consensus on its symptoms, causes or treatments. PMS is usually defined as feelings of tension and irritability that occur from two to ten days before menstruation. Other symptoms attributed to PMS include depression, anxiety, anger, indecisiveness, impatience and insomnia, as well as breast tenderness, constipation, headache and bloating.

Estimates of women with PMS range from 20% to 90%. Most researchers agree that about 5% to 10% of these women experience premenstrual discomfort severe enough to interfere with normal work or social function.

The cause of PMS is unclear, but a wide range of treatments are available. Exercise, vitamin supplements, diets restricting sugar and salt, tranquilizers and counseling have all had some success with individual women.

■ **Toxic shock syndrome (TSS)** is not directly related to the menstrual cycle. This rare condition is related to the use of high-absorbency tampons during the menstrual period.

TSS is caused by a bacterium that lives in dark, moist areas of the body, such as the vagina, throat or rectum. When the bacteria grow, they produce toxins that cause high fevers, headache, mental confusion, rashes, vomiting, diarrhea, shock, and peeling skin on the palms of the hands and soles of the feet. These symptoms indicate TSS.

Currently scientists believe that the best way for women to avoid TSS is not to use tampons continuously during their periods, and when tampons are used, to change them at least every six hours. Following these simple guidelines and seeking prompt medical attention should any symptoms occur can significantly reduce the danger of TSS.

Sexuality

Female Sexual Response

Sexual arousal affects the whole body. Men and women have many responses to sexual excitement, although the responses differ in timing and degree. In both men and women, sexual stimulation increases heart and breathing rates. Both men and women experience muscle contractions and blood congestion.

In women, blood congestion occurs in the breasts and nipples and the external genitals. The nipples grow erect and the breasts enlarge. The vagina lubricates and enlarges. The glans of the clitoris swells slightly. The uterus increases in size and contracts rhythmically during orgasm.

NOCTURNAL ORGASM

Although nocturnal orgasm for men is well known, about half of all women have orgasms during sleep, too. Women seem to experience nocturnal orgasms more frequently between the ages of thirty and fifty, but adolescents and older women have sleeping orgasms as well.

Problems of the Female Sexual Organs

Possible problems of the female sexual organs include:
- vaginitis
- breast cancer
- cervical cancer
- ovarian cancer
- uterine cancer
- ovarian cysts
- endometriosis

■ **Vaginitis** describes vaginal inflammation and infections caused by a variety of organisms. Some of these organisms are naturally present in the body and others are sexually transmitted. General symptoms include itching, pain, burning, smelly discharge and discomfort with intercourse. Vaginitis is usually treated with antibiotics.

■ Breast tissue is one of the most common sites of cancer in women. **Breast cancer** is the second leading cause of death in women (lung cancer is the first); however, when diagnosed and treated early, survival rates are higher than 90%.

No one knows what causes breast cancer. Some risk factors seem to predispose women to develop the disease. The most important of these factors are

- a family history of breast cancer, especially in a mother or sister
- a previous cancer in one breast
- being over age 45
- never having been pregnant

Women discover most breast lumps themselves. Most lumps are not cancer, but there's no way to tell without closer examination. Monthly self-examination can help women find breast lumps early. A specialized X-ray procedure, a *mammogram*, is recommended annually for women at high risk for breast cancer.

■ The cervix is a susceptible site for **cervical cancer**. A virus is the probable cause of this cancer. Risk factors include:
- frequent intercourse at an early age, especially with many different partners
- vaginal herpes infection
- human papilloma virus infection (genital warts)
- many pregnancies
- poor prenatal and after-pregnancy care

Cervical cancer is usually without symptoms until the disease is well advanced. Regular gynecological screening, including a Pap test, is the best way to identify cancer in its early stages.

- **Ovarian cancer** is rare, but because it is hard to detect early, it is often fatal. Childless women are at greatest risk. Women who already have cancer of the breast, intestines or rectum also appear to be at greater risk.

- There is no known cause for **uterine cancer,** a type of slow-growing cancer that starts in the endometrium and invades the uterine wall. Risk factors include high blood pressure, diabetes and, possibly, use of estrogen hormones.

- **Ovarian cysts,** fluid-filled sacs, can occur at any age and are very common. Usually cysts produce no symptoms; sometimes a firm, painless swelling appears in the abdomen, or a woman may have pain during sexual intercourse. Occasionally, cysts can grow large and can interfere with ovarian function or press on the bladder.

   Ovarian cysts seldom require any treatment. Some disappear on their own within a month or two. If a cyst is painful, it can be drained or removed.

- **Endometriosis** occurs when endometrial tissue grows someplace other than the uterus. Fragments may grow in the ovaries, cervix, lymph glands, abdominal wall, fallopian tubes, bladder, vagina or other locations. Because the tissue is endometrial, it responds to hormonal cues during the menstrual cycle.

Each month, the fragments bleed like the lining of the uterus. But because the fragments are embedded in other organs, the menstrual blood cannot escape. Instead, blood blisters form that irritate the surrounding tissue.

The symptoms vary depending on the organs involved, but painful periods that last a long time are the most common. The condition is found in women between the ages of 25 and 40, particularly those who have not had children.

BREAST SELF-EXAM

All women should learn to examine their breasts for lumps and other changes. The self-examination should be performed at about the same point in each menstrual cycle. During or after a shower or bath, when the skin is wet and slippery, is a good time to perform the examination.

The breasts should be probed with the fingers, moving methodically around the breast, to feel for any unusual lumps. The same examination should be conducted while the woman lies flat on her back. Women should also look at their breasts in a mirror to check for any changes in shape or outline and check the nipples for any secretions.

Regular self-exam can help a woman become familiar with the normal feel of her breasts, so she will recognize any changes. A woman should contact her doctor at once about any changes.

Sexuality

1-MINUTE FACTS

■ The female external sexual organs are the mons pubis, labia majora, labia minora, clitoris and vaginal opening, collectively called the vulva.

■ The major female reproductive organs are located inside the body. They are the vagina, uterus, fallopian tubes and ovaries.

■ Menstruation is a normal part of the female life cycle, beginning at puberty and ending at menopause.

■ The menstrual process has four phases triggered by changing levels of hormones.

Male Sexual Anatomy and Physiology

Myth: Males produce only male hormones and females produce only female hormones.

Fact: Because of the popular definition of androgens as male hormones and estrogens as female hormones, people mistakenly assume that humans produce one or the other depending on whether they are male or female. In fact, men and women have different amounts of the same hormones.

The External Organs

Unlike women, most of a man's sexual system is outside the body cavity. The most obvious external parts are the penis and scrotum.

■ The **penis** is a tubular organ with an average length of from two and a half to four inches (6.4–9.5 cm) when flaccid. During erection, most penises are about six inches long. Penises, like other body parts, vary in shape, color, skin texture and sensitivity.

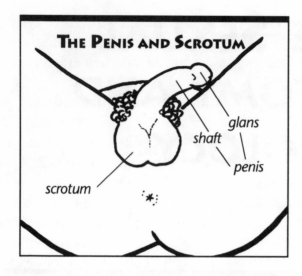

Male external sexual organs include the penis and scrotum.

The penis consists of nerves, blood vessels, fibrous tissue and three parallel cylinders of spongy tissues covered by a skin sheath. The are no bones or muscles within the penis itself, although a network of muscles around its base helps eject urine and semen from the urethra.

A portion of the penis, known as the *root*, is inside the pelvic cavity. The root is attached to the pelvic bone. The larger *shaft* hangs away from the body and is tipped by a smooth acorn-shaped head called the *glans*. The slightly raised ridge separating the glans from the shaft is called the *corona*.

Running the length of the penis are three chambers of erectile tissue. The two on the top are called the *corpora cavernosa* or *cavernous bodies*. The third chamber, known as the *corpus spongiosum*, runs along the underside of the penis and contains the *urethra*; this spongy tissue also forms the penile tip, called the *glans*. The urethra, the tube that eliminates urine from the bladder, also runs the length of the penis.

The three chambers are similar in structure. They all contain many cavities and blood vessels. During sexual arousal, the cavities fill with blood, which causes an erection.

The penis is covered with thin, loose, hairless skin connected to the shaft just behind the glans. The skin folds over and forms a hood over the glans known as the *foreskin*. The fold covers the entire glans in some men, but only a portion in others.

Under the foreskin are small glands that produce a substance called *smegma*. Usually the foreskin can be drawn back, or retracted. The glans should be washed with the foreskin retracted every day. The accumulation of dirt and smegma can be a fertile medium for bacterial growth, which could result in serious, painful infection. *Circumcision* is the surgical removal of the foreskin.

SHOULD BOYS BE CIRCUMCISED?

Circumcision, surgical removal of the foreskin covering the glans of the penis, is a common practice around the world. About half of all males are circumcised.

Sometimes circumcision is done for religious purposes, as in Islam and Judaism. Some cultures use the procedure as a rite of passage into manhood at puberty. Among Western countries, only the United States continues to have high rates of circumcision; it is becoming relatively rare in Canada and Europe.

In 1975, the American Pediatric Society concluded there is no valid medical reason for routine circumcision. Many insurance companies and some state and federal medical programs no longer cover the cost of the procedure. As a result, there has been a decrease in the number of newborn American boys who are circumcised.

HEALTH FACTS

The entire length of the penis is sensitive to physical stimulation, but the glans and corona contain a high concentration of nerve endings, which make them very sensitive to touch and temperature.

The penis is the male organ of sexual intercourse. It is important for reproduction because it delivers the sperm inside the female. It also serves to eliminate body wastes through urination. These functions cannot occur at the same time.

■ The **scrotum** is a loose, wrinkled bag of skin, sparsely covered with hair, which holds the testicles. It has a layer of muscle fibers that contract involuntarily. When the environment is warm, the scrotum relaxes, which allows the testicles to stay cool; in the cold, the scrotum contracts and pulls the testicles close to the body to keep them warm.

This is an important function because sperm production occurs best within a very narrow temperature range. The scrotum also contracts during exercise or sexual arousal, probably as a reflex to protect the testicles from injury.

The Internal Organs

There are a number of other sexual structures within the penis, scrotum and abdominal cavity. These include:

- testes
- epididymis
- vas deferens
- urethra
- prostate
- seminal vesicles
- Cowper's glands

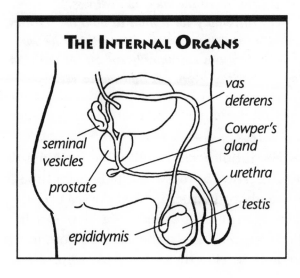

THE INTERNAL ORGANS

vas deferens

Cowper's gland

seminal vesicles

prostate

urethra

testis

epididymis

The internal male sexual organs are located within the penis, scrotum and abdominal cavity.

■ The **testes** are the male *gonads*, similar to the female ovaries. The two ball-like structures are about equal in size (two inches or 5 cm) and weigh about an ounce each. One testis, or *testicle*, will be slightly heavier and hang lower than the other in the scrotal sac.

Each testis is encased in a tight sheath that extends into it, dividing it into sections. Each section is packed with *seminiferous tubules*, threadlike structures in which sperm are produced and stored. The tubules are so small and tightly coiled that if they were unwound and laid end to end they would stretch more than a quarter of a mile (500 m). Between every two tubules, there are specialized *Leydig* or *interstitial cells*, which produce *testosterone*, the hormone responsible for male secondary sex characteristics and sexual interest and function.

WHAT'S IN A NAME?

The word **testes***, like its lexical cousin* **testimony***,*
comes from a Latin word meaning to "witness."
In ancient Rome, it was customary for a man to hold his testicles
when swearing an oath or giving evidence at a trial. If he was
found to be lying, the authorities customarily cut off his testicles.
Women, having no testicles, were not allowed to testify.

■ The seminiferous tubules empty into the **epididymis**, a tightly coiled tube. The 15- to 20-foot (4.5–6 m) tube folds to form a comma-shaped structure that curves over the top of each testicle. Sperm cells spend several weeks in this tube while they mature. It is a transport structure in which sperm mature and develop their ability to swim.

■ The **vas deferens** refers to two 17-inch (43 cm) tubes that lead from the epididymis to the *seminal vesicles*, where they form the ejaculatory ducts that empty into the urethra. Each vas travels upward in the scrotal sac, then enters the abdominal cavity, where it loops over the bladder. The vas can be felt through the top of the scrotum on each side. With a small incision, a physician can cut the vas so sperm can no longer pass through to the rest of the system. This surgery, called a *vasectomy*, makes a man sterile.

Sexuality

- The **urethra** starts at the bladder and runs through the penis to its end. It carries urine and semen out of the body, but these two substances do not mix. During sexual arousal, a valve, or *sphincter*, closes off the bladder so urine cannot pass.

- The **prostate gland,** located just below the bladder, is about the size and shape of a golf ball, with the urethra running through it. The prostate secretes a thin, milky fluid that makes up about 30% of the semen ejaculate. The prostate is small at birth, enlarges at puberty, and generally shrinks in old age. However, it may become diseased and enlarge enough to interfere with urination.

  The prostate produces a portion of the semen, which helps sperm to swim and, to some degree, protects them from the acid environment of the vagina.

- **Seminal vesicles** are two pouches located just above and to each side of the prostate. Each three-inch (7.5 cm) vesicle or sac produces a mucuslike substance that is high in fructose and protein. The sticky, yellow liquid is called *seminal fluid,* and it comprises about 70% of the semen. The fluid provides nutrients for the sperm, improves their *motility* (ability to swim) and improves their survival in the female reproductive tract.

- **Cowper's glands,** also known as the *bulbourethral glands,* are two pea-sized glands located just below the prostate. They are attached by a duct to each side of the urethra. During sexual arousal, the Cowper's glands secrete a clear, sticky fluid that appears at the tip of the penis before ejaculation. Although the exact function of this liquid is not known, scientists believe it lubricates the urethra, removes urine and neutralizes acidity.

Although this fluid is not semen, it does contain sperm about 25% of the time. Some unplanned pregnancies, particularly among couples who use withdrawal as a birth control method, have been attributed to this pre-ejaculate fluid. If a couple's contraceptive choice is condoms, the condom must be rolled onto the penis before any vaginal contact.

Sperm Development

Boys are not born with sperm. Beginning at puberty, sperm are manufactured in the seminiferous tubules within the testes. Sperm production, called *spermatogenesis*, takes place in all the tubules at the same time, so generations of sperm are made in waves. Sperm that are fully formed move into the epididymis, where they mature. The process takes approximately 64 days and continues without interruption throughout the rest of a man's lifetime.

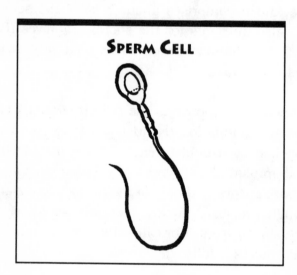

SPERM CELL

Each sperm cell has a head, midpiece and tail.

Human sperm are very tiny—about 24 thousandths of an inch (60 microns) long. They cannot be seen without a microscope. Each has a head, midpiece and tail. The head contains the chromosomes. The midpiece contains the energy-producing part of the cell. The tail whips around like a propeller to move the sperm forward.

Male Sexual Response

The stages of the male sexual response include erection and ejaculation.

■ **Erection** is controlled by the autonomic nervous system. During sexual arousal, the nerves in the spinal cord are stimulated, which triggers the arteries in the tissues in the penis to expand, dramatically increasing blood flow. The veins leading from the penis do not expand and cannot drain the inflowing blood, which accumulates in the spongy chambers, causing an erection.

The response can take as little as a few seconds or occur gradually over a longer period of time. The penis will stay erect until the brain causes the arteries to return to their normal size.

Males are able to have erections from birth. The erection reflex is involuntary; it does not require any thought on the part of the individual.

There are two types of erection. A *reflexogenic* erection is caused by physical stimulation of the penis. A *psychogenic* erection occurs in response to psychological triggers without any direct physical contact.

It is normal for all males to experience erections during the dreaming stage (REM) of sleep. Dream content may or may not be sexual. Erections can result from fantasy, sights, smells, sounds or anxiety. Erection without sexual stimuli is common in adolescence. Psychogenic erections are controlled by erection centers in the midspinal cord.

WHAT ABOUT WET DREAMS?

Wet dreams are orgasms with ejaculation that occur during sleep. In males, wet dreams, or nocturnal emissions, begin during puberty and are often, but not always, related to erotic dreams. Sleeping orgasms occur most frequently during late adolescence and the early twenties, but can happen at any age after puberty.

■ **Ejaculation** is the process in which semen is expelled through the penis to the outside of the body. It is controlled by the same portions of the spinal cord that regulate the erection response. Ejaculation is the most visible sign of postpubertal male orgasm, but it is not the same thing, since men can train themselves not to ejaculate but still experience orgasm. Before puberty, boys commonly experience orgasm without ejaculation.

Ejaculation has two stages.

• During the first phase, **seminal emission**, the muscles of the prostate, seminal vesicles and vas deferens contract, pouring their contents into the urethra. Men experience a feeling that orgasm is inevitable.

- The **expulsion** phase is characterized by vigorous contractions in the muscles around the root of the penis, other muscles in the pelvic region and and the ejaculatory ducts that expel the semen. A valve shuts off the bladder so urine cannot mix with the semen and semen can't flow backwards into the bladder.

    Semen leaves the penis in spurts relative to the muscular contractions and empties directly into the urethra.

Problems of the Male Sexual Organs

Possible problems of the male sexual organs include:
- cryptorchidism
- phimosis
- testicular torsion
- epididymitis
- hydrocele
- varicocele
- testicular cancer
- prostate cancer
- penis cancer
- sperm abnormalities

■ **Cryptorchidism (undescended testicles):** During fetal development, the testes develop in the abdominal cavity of the male fetus. About two months before birth, the testicles migrate into the scrotal sac through a passageway called the *inguinal canal.* In 2% to 4% of male births, one or both testes have failed to descend. This failure to descend is called cryptorchidism.

In most cases, the testicles will descend by themselves before puberty. If they don't, the man will be sterile because the high temperature inside the body prohibits sperm production. He is also more likely to develop testicular cancer. To prevent these risks, most boys with undescended testicles are treated with surgery and/or hormones before age five.

■ **Phimosis:** In this condition, the foreskin is so tight that it cannot be retracted to expose the penile glans. Phimosis cannot usually be identified in boys under five or six because the foreskin is normally tight. Most commonly, diagnosis occurs at puberty when the penis has grown in size and erection is extremely painful or impossible because of the foreskin. Circumcision corrects the problem.

■ **Testicular torsion:** This rare condition occurs when the testicle twists out of its normal position, causing a kink in the vas deferens and the blood vessels that run alongside it. Torsion most often occurs during adolescence, but it can happen at any age from trauma or without any clear cause.

Torsion is extremely painful. Blood flow is interrupted, so the scrotum swells and becomes tender. Torsion can cause permanent damage to the sperm-producing parts of the testicle, so prompt treatment is important.

■ **Epididymitis:** Inflammation of the epididymis can be caused by an infection that spreads from the urethra back into the sperm storage area. Symptoms include a hot, painful swelling on the top or back of the testicles, followed a few hours later by swelling and stiffening of the scrotum.

The most common cause of the disorder is *chlamydia*, a bacterium passed from one person to another during sexual contact. Antibiotics will usually cure the infection, but both partners must be treated or it will recur.

- **Hydrocele:** Each testicle is enclosed in a fibrous sheath. Between the sheath and testicle, there is just enough fluid for good lubrication. Sometimes, however, too much fluid collects around the testicle, forming a soft, usually painless swelling called a hydrocele. Hydroceles are harmless and quite common, especially in older men.

- **Varicocele:** Like other areas of the body rich in blood vessels, the veins that drain the testicles occasionally become overstretched, or distended. Varicocele is a mild form of varicose veins with no apparent cause. Wearing tight-fitting underwear or an athletic supporter relieves discomfort.

- **Testicular cancer:** Although it is relatively rare, this is the most common cancer in men ages 29 to 35. It can be cured if it is treated early. Men should perform testicular self-examination monthly.

TESTICULAR SELF-EXAM

Young men, beginning in high school, should learn to perform testicular self-exam monthly. The best time to perform the exam is after a warm shower or bath, when the muscles of the scrotum are relaxed and the skin covering the testicles is loose.

The testicle is examined by grasping it through the skin and rolling it gently between the thumb and first two fingers. The surface of the testicle should feel smooth except for a small raised area at the back, which is the epididymis. Any enlargement, hardening, lump or other change in the testicles should be checked by a physician.

- **Prostate cancer:** Only lung and skin cancers are more common than prostate cancer in men. Although nearly 5% of all men will get the disease, it is very uncommon before age 60, and it progresses very slowly. When the disease is identified early, treatment is very effective.

- **Penis cancer:** The cause of this rare but life-threatening cancer is not known. Many men who get it, however, are uncircumcised and have a history of poor hygiene. Uncircumcised men who wash the foreskin and glans have very little risk of developing the disease.

- **Sperm abnormalities:** Low sperm count is the most common cause of male infertility, the inability to father a child. Less than 40 million sperm per cubic centimeter is below normal, and less than 20 million makes pregnancy very unlikely. Some men produce enough sperm, but the sperm do not mature fully or cannot swim properly.

    Testicular injury, infection (especially adult mumps), radiation, hormone disorders, undescended testes and birth defects can interfere with sperm production. Use of alcohol, cigarettes, marijuana, narcotics and other drugs can reduce sperm count. Since sperm production is sensitive to temperature, some scientists believe that frequent and prolonged use of hot tubs, saunas and other hot environments can lower production or cause a higher rate of malformations.

1-Minute Facts

■ Most of the male reproductive system is outside the body, including the penis and scrotum.

■ Male internal organs include the testes, epididymis, vas deferens, urethra, prostate, seminal vesicles and Cowper's glands.

■ Males begin to manufacture sperm at puberty and continue throughout their lives.

■ Male erection is controlled by the autonomic nervous system and is common during REM sleep.

■ Ejaculation is the process in which semen is expelled through the penis.

PREGNANCY AND BIRTH

At conception, a single fertilized cell is formed when a male's sperm joins with a female's egg. The egg and sperm are known as *gametes,* and the fusion of these two parent cells to produce a new individual of the next generation is called *sexual reproduction.*

■ **Chromosomes** are structures in cells that contain genetic information. Each species has a different number of chromosomes. Humans have 23 pairs, for a total of 46 chromosomes. Chromosomes are classified into two types: 44 *autosomes,* which carry information about how bodies look and function, and two sex chromosomes, which determine genetic sex. The sex chromosomes are called X and Y. A pair of X chromosomes (XX) produces a female, and a mixed pair (XY) produces a male.

Chromosomes are paired in every human cell except the gametes, which carry only 23 chromosomes, or one-half of each pair of chromosomes. Each of the female's eggs has 22 autosomes and one X chromosome; each sperm from the male has 22 autosomes and either an X or a Y chromosome. If an egg is fertilized by a sperm cell with the X chromosome, the fetus is genetically female. If an egg is fertilized by a sperm cell with the Y chromosome, the fetus is genetically male.

Occasionally, eggs and sperm contain abnormal numbers of sex chromosomes, either too few or too many. If a fetus contained two X chromosomes and a single Y chromosome (XXY), the sex would still be male. If a fetus had only one X chromosome and no Y, the sex would be female. However, a fetus with a single Y chromosome and no X would die.

Alternations in the number of chromosomes is not limited to sex chromosomes. Scientists have identified more than seventy conditions in both males and females that result from the addition or loss of chromosomes, including Down syndrome. An extra chromosome can produce a functional individual with Down syndrome.

A medical test called *amniocentesis* can detect chromosomal and other fetal abnormalities. However, this test is only recommended in high-risk situations.

Conception

Ovulation occurs about 14 days before the menstrual period begins. At ovulation, the egg leaves the ovary and is swept toward one of the fallopian tubes by the waving fimbriae. Once it enters the tube, the egg begins its trip to the uterus. If it is fertilized, this trip will take about five days; if not, the egg will disintegrate in about 48 hours.

During intercourse, a male will ejaculate about a teaspoonful of semen, containing 100 to 600 million sperm, into a female's vagina. In the vagina, most of the semen is left behind as the sperm begin to swim toward the uterus by lashing their tails.

Many of the sperm are killed or get lost in the acidic vaginal environment, but about half will find the cervix, swim through the mucus in its opening, enter the uterus and head for the fallopian tubes. About half the remaining sperm never reach the egg because they swim up the wrong fallopian tube. But, after a few hours, about 2,000 sperm are moving up the tube containing the egg. Only about fifty of these sperm ever find the egg.

Fertilization must take place in the outer third of the fallopian tube near the ovary. The egg sends out signals attracting the remaining sperm to its surface, where they release the digestive enzymes stored in their heads. By a mechanism which is not yet understood, one sperm's genetic material is selected and sucked into the egg. Once this has occurred, the egg's surface changes, making it impossible for any other sperm to get through.

At fertilization, the sperm's 23 chromosomes merge with the egg's 23 chromosomes to form a new cell containing the 46 chromosomes typical of human cells. The fertilized egg, now called a *zygote*, continues to move toward the uterus. After about thirty hours, it divides into two cells, then four, then eight. This division continues until the zygote becomes a hollow ball of cells, or *morula*, by the time it reaches the uterus three days later.

This little ball of cells surrounding a fluid-filled center, now known as a *blastocyst*, floats around in the uterus until, sometime between the fifth and seventh day after ovulation, it attaches to the endometrium. This step is called *implantation*; it is the true physiological beginning of pregnancy.

TREATING INFERTILITY

Modern technology has developed new techniques for treating infertility. In addition to surgery to repair reproductive problems such as blocked fallopian tubes, treatments include *artificial insemination* and *in vitro fertilization*.

In artificial insemination, a male donor provides sperm that are inserted into a woman's vagina in a simple, painless procedure.

In vitro fertilization involves removing an egg from a woman's ovary, fertilizing it with her partner's sperm in a laboratory, and then implanting it in the woman's uterus.

Pregnancy

Pregnancy is divided into three equal periods of three months, called *trimesters*. For the first eight weeks, the organism is called an *embryo*; for the rest of gestation, it is called a *fetus*.

The average length of a human pregnancy is 266 days. Babies born before the 36th week are considered premature. Today, babies born up to two months premature, and sometimes slightly more, can survive.

The First Trimester

The first eight weeks of pregnancy are critical because most of the major organ systems are formed during this time. Development proceeds at an amazing rate. The ball of cells implanted on the uterine wall differentiates into the following three layers from which the body systems will develop:

- The **ectoderm** forms the nervous system and the skin.
- The **endoderm** forms digestive and respiratory systems.
- The **mesoderm** forms muscle, skeleton, connective tissues and reproductive and circulatory systems.

By the third week, the embryo is just 1/12 of an inch (0.2 cm) long, but the head is visible, with the beginnings of eyes and ears. The brain, other parts of the central nervous system and backbone are starting to form.

From the fourth through the eighth weeks, the external body parts develop. Eyes, ears, arms, hands, fingers, legs, feet and toes are complete by the tenth week. The primitive heart and beginnings of the digestive system are in place. Bones are becoming hard with calcium.

By the seventh week, the liver, lungs, pancreas, kidneys and intestines are functioning in a limited way. The *gonads*, the ovaries or testes, have formed, but males and females are not easily distinguished.

While these changes are occurring, another group of cells is beginning to form a lifeline between the embryo and the mother. By the end of the first trimester, these cells will have differentiated into the *placenta*, which supplies nutrients and oxygen to the fetus and removes its waste.

This transport takes place via blood vessels in the *umbilical cord*, which is formed during the fifth week of pregnancy and will reach an average length of 20 inches (55 cm) by the end of pregnancy. The cord connects the fetal circulatory system to the placenta.

The fetal blood comes very close to the mother's but does not mix, because the placental membrane keeps them separate. The membrane does allow nutrients, hormones, electrolytes and antibodies to pass.

The membrane blocks some agents that may be harmful to the fetus but not all. Most drugs, including alcohol and nicotine, will pass directly through the membrane from the mother to the fetus. In some cases, infectious agents can cross the placental barrier. Rubella (German measles) and HIV are two examples of infections that can be transmitted through the placenta.

During the third month, fingernails, toenails, hair follicles and eyelids appear. The limbs become more proportional to the rest of the body, and the sex organs are recognizable. At the end of the twelfth week, the fetus is about four inches (10 cm) long and looks like a miniature human baby. From this point on, development is mainly refining and enlarging the structures already in place.

DRUG USE IN PREGNANCY

Almost every drug used by the mother crosses the placental membrane and enters the fetal bloodstream. Many drugs are toxic to the fetus, especially early in pregnancy. They can cause a variety of birth defects, depending on how long and how much was used. Some common drugs that affect the fetus include the following:

Drug	Effects
aspirin	bleeding
antibiotics	respiratory problems, deafness
birth control pills	limb defects, genital malformations
accutane	face and heart defects
anti-cancer drugs	death

Other Drugs

Drugs such as cocaine, heroin, barbiturates and amphetamines can cause miscarriage and stillbirth and a large number of other problems for a newborn, including:
- premature birth
- low birth weight
- underdeveloped brain and nervous system
- genital and urinary tract malformations
- addiction and withdrawal symptoms
- convulsions/seizures
- breathing problems

Smoking

Smoking cigarettes is dangerous, too. Women who smoke have a greater risk for miscarriage, premature birth and complications during pregnancy and labor. Their babies are often underweight. Low birth weight may result in children having behavior problems, lower intelligence, poor motor skills and related disorders.

Alcohol

Alcohol can cause severe physical, mental and behavioral problems, which are referred to as *fetal alcohol syndrome*. Possible defects include:

- alcohol addiction
- pre- and postnatal growth deficiencies
- underdeveloped brain and nervous system
- facial abnormalities, particularly affecting the eyes
- heart problems
- mental retardation
- irritability and hyperactivity
- learning disabilities

The Second Trimester

A pregnant woman can feel the fetus moving at about the fourteenth week. This fluttering is called "quickening." The fetal lips are developing and sucking motions are beginning. By the eighteenth week, a physician can hear the fetal heartbeat.

The fetus opens its eyes at week 20 and is sensitive to light and sounds by week 24. Its skin is wrinkled and covered by fine hair. The fetus is very active at this point.

At the end of the second trimester, the fetus weighs about two pounds (880 g) and is 14 inches (35.5 cm) long.

The Third Trimester

At the beginning of the third trimester, the fetus loses its hair covering. Fat deposits, which will give the baby a chubby appearance, form under the skin.

During the seventh month, the fetus will usually move into a head-down position in the uterus. In the last two months, the fetus grows rapidly in its cramped quarters. By the end of the eighth month, it weighs about five and a half pounds (2500 g). At birth, the average full-term baby weighs seven and a half pounds (3300 g) and is twenty inches (50 cm) long.

Birth

The actual mechanism that triggers *labor*, the rhythmic uterine contractions that result in the delivery of the child, the placenta and fetal membranes, is not known. However, it is probably related to hormonal levels in the mother's blood.

Labor is divided into three stages:

■ **Stage 1:** The first stage of labor is usually the longest, lasting an average of 15 hours for first pregnancies and eight hours for subsequent deliveries. The primary task of the first stage contractions, which begin 15 to 20 minutes apart and gradually occur more frequently with greater intensity, is to dilate or open the cervix to about four inches (10 cm) in diameter.

■ **Stage 2:** Stage 2 labor begins when the cervix is fully dilated and ends when the baby is born. It can last for a few minutes or several hours. If the amniotic sac has not already broken, the birth attendant will deliberately rupture the membranes. Once the baby is outside the mother's body and is breathing on its own, the umbilical cord is cut. Often, the newborn is placed at the mother's breast for its first meal and to begin the bonding process. The suckling action of the newborn helps stimulate the onset of the third stage of labor.

■ **Stage 3:** Stage 3 is the delivery of the *afterbirth*, which includes the placenta and the fetal membranes. The uterus continues to contract and begins to shrink in size. Some bleeding may continue for several days after the delivery.

1-Minute Facts

- Sexual reproduction refers to the fusion of the male sperm and the female egg to produce a new individual.

- Chromosomes are structures in cells that contain genetic information.

- Fertilization occurs when the male's sperm enters the female's egg; it must take place in a fallopian tube, near the ovary.

- Pregnancy is divided into three equal periods of three months, called trimesters.

- The first eight weeks of pregnancy are critical because most of the major organ systems are formed.

- During the second trimester, the fetus becomes very active.

- During the third trimester, the fetus grows very rapidly.

- Labor is divided into three stages: dilation of the cervix, followed by birth and then delivery of the afterbirth.

Sexuality

CONTRACEPTION

MYTH: Douching after intercourse is a safe, effective method of birth control.

Fact: Viable sperm can sometimes be found in the fallopian tubes 90 seconds after ejaculation. Douching, or rinsing out the vagina with liquids, has no effect on sperm already inside the uterus. Some evidence suggests that douching can push sperm into the cervix.

Even before humans understood the relationship between intercourse and procreation, they tried to devise ways to prevent pregnancy. Probably the oldest contraceptive practice is withdrawal, in which a man removes his penis from the woman's vagina before ejaculation. The earliest account of this method is found in the Bible's Old Testament story of Onan, who "let his seed be lost on the ground."

The ancient Egyptians used various vaginal pastes which acted as both barriers and spermicides. The early Romans and Greeks used herbal potions, sterilization and abortion to reduce the birth rate.

Gabriello Fallopius, the Italian anatomist and discoverer of the fallopian tubes, published the first description of condoms in 1564. Made from animal intestines, condoms were used to prevent pregnancy and the sexual transmission of disease.

By 1900, virtually all contraceptive methods now in use, except hormonal methods, were used. Vaginal barriers like the diaphragm and cap were used in Germany by the 1820s. Charles Goodyear's discovery of the rubber vulcanization process in 1839 made condoms widely available.

Vasectomy was practiced in the nineteenth century, and the first female sterilization by cutting the fallopian tubes was performed by an Ohio surgeon in 1881. In the 1860s, a Scottish physician, James Young Simpson, described a method of vacuum aspiration for abortions in early pregnancy.

In the 1920s, a German physician reported that silk or silver rings inside the uterus prevented pregnancy at an astonishing rate of 98%, but his work was generally ignored. Not until stainless steel and plastic devices were developed in the 1950s did this method gain popularity.

Before the middle of the twentieth century, the scientific foundations of hormonal birth control were already in place. It was known that ovulation occurred 14 days prior to the next menstruation, and that the entire cycle was controlled by hormones, of which estrogen had been isolated. However, negative public reactions prevented further research until the 1960s, when the first oral contraceptives became available.

The Birth Control Movement

Margaret Sanger, a registered nurse working in the slums of New York City in the early 1900s, made family planning a global social movement. Much of Sanger's work was with poor women, old and worn out at 35 from constant childbearing. Sanger became so frustrated by the deaths of so many women from pregnancy and illegal abortions that she founded the National Birth Control League in 1914 and began publishing a magazine called *Woman Rebel*.

However, an 1873 law known as the Comstock Act made contraceptive information illegal and prohibited its distribution through the mail. When Sanger was indicted for violating the act, she fled to Europe. There she toured the first family planning clinics in Holland. When she returned to the United States in 1916, the charges that had been filed against her were dropped.

Later that year, Sanger opened a family planning clinic in Brooklyn. The clinic was shut down by the police, and Sanger was arrested and convicted on charges of "maintaining a public nuisance."

Sanger spent thirty days in jail before her conviction was overturned on appeal. In a compromise solution, family planning clinics were allowed to operate in the United States on the condition that physicians be involved in dispensing contraceptives.

In 1936, a New York court ruled that physicians could receive contraceptives through the mail if they were to be used for saving lives or promoting well-being of patients, delivering the final blow to the Comstock Act.

Contraceptive Methods

There is no such thing as a perfect contraceptive. Contraceptive devices do fail occasionally, and people sometimes fail to use the devices consistently and correctly. All contraceptive methods have some side effects or potential risks.

Abstinence

Choosing not to have intercourse, or abstinence, is the safest and most effective way to avoid pregnancy and reduce the risk of sexually transmitted disease. This method is free, requires no prescription or exam, is always available, is accepted religiously and morally, is reversible and has no side effects.

Barrier Methods

All barrier methods work on the same principle: they mechanically or chemically prevent the sperm from reaching the egg.

These forms of contraception are widely available and are used by many couples. They are quite effective, although there is a relatively high incidence of incorrect use, which raises the actual failure rate.

CONTRACEPTIVE EFFECTIVENESS

How well contraceptive methods work is measured by how often they fail: how many women out of a hundred get pregnant when a given method is used for one year.

Two rates are usually recorded. The theoretical rate is the number of failures based on perfect method performance. It is the lowest reported rate of failure in research studies.

The actual or typical failure rate accounts for human error in real-life users who do not receive the training and attention typical of research subjects.

Many couples dislike barrier methods because they must interrupt sexual activity to use them and some can be messy or otherwise unpleasant to use. However, it is possible to overcome these reactions and learn to make using barrier methods a pleasurable part of sexual activity.

■ **Spermicides** are chemical preparations that kill sperm and block the entrance to the cervix. They are sold in five basic forms: creams, jellies, foam, vaginal film and suppositories. The active ingredient in many of these products is nonoxynol-9. Spermicides do not require a prescription. They are available over the counter at grocery and drug stores and in family planning clinics.

All spermicides are placed directly in the vagina, but different products have different rules for use and effectiveness. Foams, creams and jellies come with a plastic applicator, which is filled and then inserted into the vagina and emptied. These spermicides are effective immediately, but only work for about half an hour. Suppositories and film are pushed into the vagina with the finger and must be in place for 10 to 15 minutes before they will work. Users should read the directions for use of each product carefully.

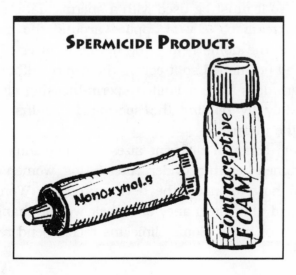

SPERMICIDE PRODUCTS

Spermicides come in a variety of forms.

Theoretically, spermicides fail only 3% of the time. Foam is the most effective form, followed by creams and jellies and finally film and suppositories.

However, these products are often used incorrectly and thus have an actual failure rate of 18% to 21%. Failures occur when couples insert the spermicide into the vagina improperly, have intercourse a second time without using more of the product, ignore the time limits on effectiveness, or use spermicide that is out of date.

Only about 4% of women use spermicides alone. They are most effective when used with another barrier form of contraception.

The main side effect of these products is irritation of the vagina or penis, which occurs in about 5% of users. Irritation can often be eliminated by switching to another product.

Spermicides have several positive health effects. They provide some protection against sexually transmitted disease. Products with nonoxynol-9 may help prevent the transmission of HIV. Women who use them are also less susceptible to vaginal infections.

■ The **diaphragm** is a round, shallow dome of thin rubber stretched across a flexible ring. Used alone, the diaphragm is unreliable, so it must be used with a spermicidal cream or jelly. The cream or jelly is applied around the inner rim and inside the dome before the device is inserted in the vagina and positioned so it covers the cervix. Although the diaphragm does have a limited sperm-blocking effect, it works mainly by holding the spermicide against the entrance to the uterus.

Diaphragms come in different sizes, so they must be fitted by a trained health provider. After fitting, women are instructed in how to insert the device properly. Women must be refitted after pregnancy or if their weight changes by ten pounds or more. Some clinicians recommend refitting annually.

Sexuality

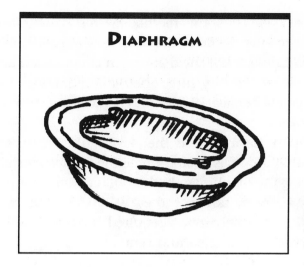

DIAPHRAGM

Diaphragms must be used with a spermicidal cream or jelly.

The diaphragm can be inserted up to two hours before intercourse and must be left in place six to eight hours after intercourse. If it is worn for more than two hours before intercourse or for repeated acts of intercourse, the device should be left in place and more spermicide added to the vagina. Diaphragms should not be left in the vagina for more than 12 hours.

When fitted and inserted properly, neither partner can feel the diaphragm during intercourse. The device can be washed and reused. About 4% of U.S. women and 4 million women throughout the world use the diaphragm for contraception. Under perfect conditions, the failure rate for the device is just 2% or less.

However, diaphragm use is dependent on a woman's remembering and being motivated to use it. The device can slip out of position during sex, especially if it is not well fitted. Diaphragms can also develop tiny undetectable holes, sometimes due to using Vaseline or other products that cause the rubber to deteriorate, which allow sperm to enter the uterus.

Thus, the actual failure rate of the diaphragm is 6% to 20%. Used with a condom, effectiveness increases to almost 100%.

The only side effects of this method are a possible allergy to the rubber or spermicide or the chance of introducing an infection into the vagina if the diaphragm is not clean. Both of these problems are very rare. The diaphragm does offer protection against cervical cancer and some sexually transmitted diseases.

Once women learn to use the device, they ordinarily have no trouble. However, some women feel uncomfortable about inserting the diaphragm in the vagina. Many couples, unless they know in advance they will be having intercourse, dislike the interruption required to insert the diaphragm. Some find insertion and removal messy.

■ The **cervical cap** fits snugly over the cervix and is held in place by suction. It prevents pregnancy by blocking the entrance to the cervix. It can be used with a spermicide, but the spermicide is not required.

The cervical cap, a popular contraceptive in Europe, has only been used in the United States since 1988. It is made of soft rubber and is shaped like a thimble.

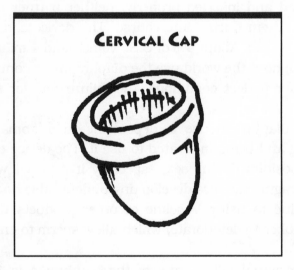

CERVICAL CAP

Cervical caps do not require the use of spermicides.

Sexuality

The cap comes in four different sizes, so it must be fitted. It is harder to learn how to insert the cap than a diaphragm. FDA guidelines say the cap should stay in place no longer than 48 hours; however, some data suggest it can be worn longer without problems.

The cervical cap is comparable to the diaphragm in effectiveness. Actual failure rates range from 6% to 20%. Some studies show the cap sometimes fails because it can pop off during intercourse.

The cap's suction may cause some erosion of the cervical tip. The cap also has been linked to abnormal Pap smears in a small number of users, but it is unclear if these are minor microscopic changes due to inflammation or may in fact be indicators of precancerous conditions. Women who have abnormal Pap smears or anatomical cervical abnormalities should not use the cap.

Some men say they can feel the cap during intercourse, and it causes them discomfort. However, this occurs very infrequently. About 20% of users complain about vaginal odor, probably caused by normal cervical secretions that can't leave the body.

The cap has three main advantages: it does not change a woman's hormone levels or any other body functions; it permits more sexual spontaneity; it is not messy to use.

■ The **contraceptive sponge** is somewhat like a disposable diaphragm. The sponge, which is inserted in the vagina and covers the cervix, is a two-by-one-inch soft polyurethane disc with a dimple in the center. It contains the spermicide nonoxynol-9. It is sold in drug stores under the brand name "Today" and does not require a prescription or fitting by a physician.

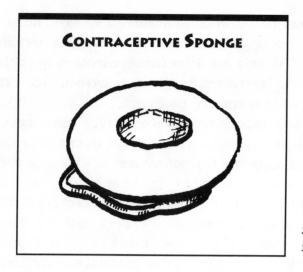

CONTRACEPTIVE SPONGE

The contraceptive sponge contains a spermicide.

Before insertion, the user must activate the spermicide with about two tablespoons of water and gently squeeze the sponge until foam appears. The sponge can be placed in the vagina up to 18 hours before intercourse; it remains effective for 24 hours without any need to apply more spermicide no matter how many times intercourse occurs during that period.

Like the diaphragm, the sponge must be left in place for six hours after intercourse. It is removed from the vagina by looping a finger into a ribbon attached to the sponge and pulling it out.

The sponge works in three ways: the spermicide kills sperm; the sponge blocks the entrance to the cervix; and the sponge material traps and absorbs sperm.

The actual failure rate during the first year of sponge use is high, about 17%. However, during the second year, actual failures are much lower, about 5%. Learning how to use the device properly and building a habit of using it every time make the difference. Like the diaphragm, using the sponge with a condom improves its effectiveness.

About 3% to 5% of users report mild irritation of the vagina or penis, probably from sensitivity to the spermicide.

The most serious health risk related to sponge use is the rare occurrence of toxic shock syndrome. This condition has occurred in one out of 4 million users, so the risk is very, very low. To avoid even this risk, women should not leave the sponge in the vagina for more than thirty hours.

There are many advantages to this contraceptive method. Since the sponge can be inserted hours before intercourse or at the last moment, it is convenient. It is easy to insert, effective for multiple acts of intercourse, inexpensive, disposable, tasteless and odorless. Neither men nor women can feel it during intercourse.

■ The **condom** is the only reliable, nonsurgical method of birth control currently in use for men. Originally, condoms were made from animal intestines or linen. Also called sheaths, rubbers or prophylactics, most modern condoms are thin, cylindrical sacs made of latex rubber.

CONDOM

Condoms, especially latex condoms, substantially reduce the risk of sexually transmitted disease.

The condom fits snugly over the erect penis. The open end has a ring of harder rubber and the closed end often has a nipple reservoir to hold the ejaculate. If the condom does not have a built-in reservoir, a half-inch should be left loose at the closed end for this purpose.

Although condoms generally come in one size, they vary in many other ways. Some are lubricated, some dry. Some are coated with spermicide and lubricant.

Condoms do not require a prescription and can be purchased in drug stores, convenience stores, gas stations, bathrooms, family planning centers and through the mail. Unopened condoms are good for about two years if they are stored away from heat. The date of manufacture is printed on the packages of all U.S. condoms.

The condom is rolled flat in its plastic or foil package. The man or his partner unrolls the condom onto the erect penis before it makes any contact with the vagina, not just before ejaculation. This helps avoid the slight risk that stray sperm may be in the pre-ejaculate fluid secreted by the Cowper's glands and the risk that the man will ejaculate before he intends to.

After ejaculation, the man should withdraw his penis from the vagina before he loses his erection, holding the condom at the base of the penis so it can't slip off or leak. If there is any leakage, spermicide should be placed in the vagina immediately. The used condom should be thrown away. If the couple decides to have intercourse again, the man should wash or wipe his penis and put on a new condom.

Latex condoms will deteriorate and are likely to break if they are used with any oil-based products. Baby oil, Vaseline, vegetable oil, hand creams and massage oils should not be used as lubricants. Materials that wash off easily with water may still be oil-based. Spermicides, K-Y Jelly or other true water-based products will not deteriorate condoms and can be used as lubricants.

U.S. and Japanese manufacturers make more than a billion condoms a year. About 10% of U.S. couples and 21% of teenage males rely on condoms for contraception.

The theoretical effectiveness of condoms is quite high, with fewer than five pregnancies per 100 couples over a year. The more accurate actual failure rate is 10% to 20%. The lower effectiveness is due mostly to inconsistent use. Couples who use condoms consistently with another method have unwanted pregnancies at a rate of only 2%.

Condoms have no health risks at all except very rare instances of irritation caused by sensitivity to the latex or lubricant. Disadvantages include interruption of sexual activity to put the condom on and lessened sensations in the penis or vagina. Some men with erectile problems have difficulty maintaining an erection while trying to put on the device.

Women often appreciate a man's willingness to take responsibility for pregnancy prevention. Men who tend to ejaculate prematurely find condoms help them delay orgasm. Condoms are not messy.

The biggest advantage in addition to contraception, however, is that condoms substantially reduce the risk of sexually transmitted disease. Natural membrane condoms block out bacterial organisms, but some have pores large enough to allow passage of viruses such as hepatitis B or HIV. Latex condoms, especially if used with a spermicide, offer excellent protection against sexually transmitted disease.

Hormonal Methods

Hormones control the reproductive processes in both men and women. Using synthetic hormones can change reproductive functioning.

Hormonal contraceptives use artificial derivatives of the natural steroid hormones *estrogen* and *progesterone* to prevent ovulation during a woman's menstrual cycle. The hormones can be taken as pills or by injection or implanted under the skin. So far, oral use has proven the most practical method.

Hormonal contraceptives are the most effective reversible birth control method available today. Properly used, they provide better than 99% protection from pregnancy. Because these methods change the body's basic functions, however, users can experience some serious side effects. On the other hand, hormones can provide some benefits that other methods do not, such as regulating the menstrual cycle.

■ **Oral contraceptives** were developed in the 1950s and received FDA approval in 1960 for sale in the United States. The availability of a method of birth control that was effective, cheap, convenient, controlled by the woman and unrelated to the act of intercourse revolutionized contraceptive practice. Today, oral contraceptives, known simply as "the pill," are used by more women than any other reversible method worldwide—more than 60 million.

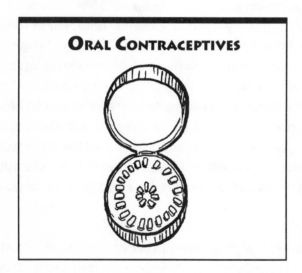

ORAL CONTRACEPTIVES

Oral contraceptives, known as "the pill," are safe and effective for most women.

Oral contraceptives contain combinations of synthetic hormones that imitate the actions of natural estrogens and progestins. They prevent ovulation because they inhibit brain production of FSH and LH, the hormones that stimulate ovulation. They also change the uterine lining in ways that make implantation difficult and cause the cervical mucus to become thicker and more acid, which blocks and kills sperm.

- **Combination pills,** the most widely used type of oral contraceptive, contain mainly progesterone with a little estrogen. They are taken once a day for 21 days. For the next seven days, the user has her menstrual period, caused by the drop in the synthetic progesterone hormone. Then she begins the next cycle of pills.

- **Sequential pills** imitated the daily changes in hormones during a woman's cycle. They prevented pregnancy, but users developed serious side effects, and these pills were taken off the market.

- **Multiphasic pills,** which contain varying amounts of hormones but at very low doses, replaced the dangerous sequential type. These pills come in two varieties, biphasic and triphasic. *Biphasic pills* provide a small amount of estrogen for the first ten days, followed by a much higher dose of progestin and the same dose of estrogen for the remainder of the cycle. *Triphasic pills* use three combinations of the hormones. Women must take the right pills in the right sequence for these types to be effective; however, when used correctly, multiphasic pills work very well.

- The **minipill** is a progestin-only preparation. It is taken every day throughout the cycle. It has fewer side effects than combination pills, but is less effective in preventing ovulation. It works mainly by changing the quality of cervical mucus. Users are also subject to more irregular menstrual bleeding.

Combination pills, including multiphasic, are the most effective method of birth control except sterilization. The theoretical failure rate among users over a year is just one-tenth of a percent. In actual use, about 3 in 100 women become pregnant while using the pill. Minipills have a theoretical failure rate of 1%, slightly higher than combination types, but in actual use they have the same rate of 3%.

All drugs can cause side effects, both bad and good. Birth control pills are no exception. However, these preparations have been studied extensively. Oral contraceptives are safe and effective for most women. Some evidence suggests that women who use the pill may receive some health benefits, such as reduced risk of osteoporosis and arthritis.

The most common negative side effects of oral contraceptives mimic those of early pregnancy: nausea, constipation, breast tenderness, minor elevations in blood pressure, swelling and skin rashes. Some women gain or lose weight, and there is an increase in vaginal secretions and an increased susceptibility to vaginal infections. These effects are usually transient, meaning they disappear after the first few cycles. For some women, however, the symptoms can appear monthly.

Less common but more serious effects of the pill include high blood pressure, headaches, diabetes and, very rarely, liver disease.

The most serious side effects of birth control pills are cardiovascular disorders. In the 1960s and 1970s, circulatory problems affected one in 1,000 pill users. These problems were directly related to high estrogen levels in early pills; all occur considerably less often today because modern pills contain very low amounts of estrogen.

There is no evidence that oral contraceptives affect subsequent fertility, although it may take several months for normal fertility to return once pills are discontinued. Pills do not affect the onset of menopause.

Finally, because the pill can be taken at any time of the day, its use does not interfere with sexual activity. For many couples, this increases spontaneity and sexual enjoyment. However, the pill provides no protection against most sexually transmitted diseases, including HIV.

■ **Injectables** and **subdermals** function in the same way as birth control pills but provide an alternative method of delivering the hormones. These methods confer protection against pregnancy from thirty days to five years by leaching controlled amounts of hormones into the body.

Injectable contraceptives are registered in more than eighty countries, including most of the developing world, the United Kingdom, Sweden, New Zealand and, most recently, the United States. Subdermal, under the skin, implants (Norplant) are also used in Europe, developing countries and the United States.

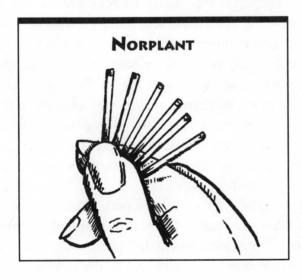

NORPLANT

Norplant, birth control capsules implanted under the skin, provides protection against pregnancy for up to five years.

Because these devices are not widely available, accurate failure rates have not been established. However, injectables so far show a failure rate of less than 1%.

Both positive and negative side effects are similar to those of oral contraceptives. Other effects may become apparent when these methods have been in use for longer periods of time.

■ **Postcoital pills,** pills that are taken after intercourse, do not prevent ovulation or fertilization. They prevent pregnancy by interfering with implantation of the fertilized egg.

Several versions of postcoital pills are available. Diethylstilbestrol, better known as DES, is a potent form of estrogen, which prevents pregnancy if given to a woman twice a day for five days beginning no later than 72 hours after unprotected intercourse.

DES causes severe nausea and vomiting. It is not currently legal for birth control purposes (although it is legally available from doctors for other uses). The drug has also been linked to birth defects and cancers in female children of women who take it if the pregnancy is not prevented. Its efficacy as a contraceptive remains questionable.

A newer postcoital pill containing a more tolerable, safer form of estrogen, sometimes combined with a progestin, is available. The first pill is taken as soon as possible after intercourse, followed by a second 12 to 72 hours later. Because the hormone content is only about four times that of oral contraceptives, nausea is much less severe. This pill is not available as a regular form of birth control; it is currently used on an emergency-need basis, usually following an event such as rape or incest.

In 1986, French researchers developed and marketed an antiprogestin drug they called RU-486. A single dose taken within ten days of a missed menstrual period will block the effects of progesterone, which sustains early pregnancy. Without progesterone, the uterine lining is shed and menstruation occurs; the embryo is lost in the menstrual flow.

Excessive bleeding and incomplete evacuation of the uterus are the most common problems associated with RU-486, occurring in about 1% of women who take the drug. Therefore, it must be used under medical supervision. The drug is completely metabolized in 48 hours and does not impair fertility.

RU-486 is approved for use in France and China. It was recently approved for testing in the United States. The drug has been the focus of controversy between factions on different sides of the abortion question.

Postcoital pills, although fairly effective, appear to fail much more often than oral contraceptives. Effectiveness is directly related to the amount of time passed since unprotected intercourse. Pills taken within 72 hours fail 7% to 9% of the time.

Intrauterine Devices

The intrauterine device, or IUD, is a flexible object, about the size of a paper clip, that is inserted into the uterus. IUDs can be made from many materials, but modern versions are plastic, shaped like a T or S, with a nylon thread attached to the bottom. Some have copper wire around them or contain synthetic progesterone, which slowly dissolves while the device is in place.

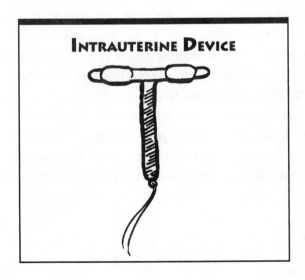

INTRAUTERINE DEVICE

Intrauterine devices can be left in place for a year or more.

IUDs come packaged in an inserter tube that is slipped through the cervix. The plastic piece is released in the uterus, the tube is removed, and the thread trails out into the vagina so the woman can check that the IUD is in place.

IUDs must be inserted and removed by a trained health professional when a woman is not pregnant and does not have an infection. Most commonly, IUDs are inserted during the menstrual period and immediately after childbirth or abortion.

The exact way IUDs prevent pregnancy is not known. Like the pill, they probably act in several ways. Inflammation of the uterine lining may prevent implantation of the fertilized egg. Abnormally high numbers of white blood cells in the uterus may destroy the egg, whether it is fertilized or not, and sperm. Chemical changes in the fallopian tubes also seem to block sperm from reaching the egg.

About 60 million women worldwide use this method, including about 35 million women in China. Only two models of IUDs are currently available in the United States, Progestacert and the Copper T380A. The Progestacert, which must be replaced annually, and the Copper T, which can be used continuously for four years, are much safer than older versions, but currently, only about 6% of U.S. women are using IUDs as their contraceptive.

IUDs are very effective if a woman can tolerate the device and it is inserted properly. A number of studies show use of the Copper T results in fewer than one pregnancy per 100 women a year, while the Progestacert has a pregnancy rate of 3% per year. However, taking into account those who discontinue the method and under-reported abortions, the actual failure rate probably approaches 6%.

IUDs do have many side effects and potential problems, the most serious of which is uterine perforation at the time of insertion. Punctures of the uterus are not common, occurring about one time per 1,000 insertions, but they can be emergency situations.

Uterine contractions can cause the device to be partially or completely expelled. About 7% of IUDs containing copper or progestin are expelled a year. Younger women and those who have never been pregnant have the highest incidence of expulsion.

The most common side effect is increased bleeding from the uterus, which affects 10% to 20% of users. Menstrual periods tend to be heavier and last longer, and spotting may occur between periods. In extreme cases, increased blood loss may lead to anemia.

Cramping may occur throughout the menstrual cycle and may be more severe during menstruation. Generally, bleeding and cramping will disappear after a few months, but in about 10% of cases it will be so severe that the IUD must be removed.

IUD users have four times the risk of pelvic infection, both during insertion and after. Bacteria, viruses and other pathogens can use the thread as a pathway from the vagina into the uterus. The infection can spread to the fallopian tubes and ovaries, which may result in infertility. About 88,000 cases of infertility were related to IUD use prior to 1985, particularly from a poorly designed device called the Dalkon Shield. IUDs provide no protection against STD and HIV.

Women who use IUDs and become pregnant have a slightly higher chance that the pregnancy will be ectopic. If a uterine pregnancy occurs, spontaneous abortion happens about half the time unless the IUD is removed.

Fertility Awareness Techniques

Popularly called *rhythm*, fertility awareness methods rely on understanding the timing of a woman's menstrual cycle. Couples learn to predict when a woman is fertile and when she's not. Fertility awareness is the only contraceptive practice accepted by some religious faiths, including the Catholic Church.

Only about 2% of women use fertility awareness methods. The theoretical failure rate of all the methods combined is 2%. The actual failure rate, however, is about 20%.

The methods are free and have no medical side-effects except pregnancy. However, they require long periods of abstinence from sexual intercourse and a high degree of cooperation from both partners.

When a combination of fertility awareness methods is used, efficacy increases. When fertility awareness is used with a barrier method, the combined ability to prevent pregnancy approaches that of the pill and other hormonal methods.

- In the **calendar method,** women count the days between menstrual periods and determine their "unsafe" or fertile time by mathematical calculations based on longest and shortest cycles. The failure rate for this method is very high, somewhere between 15% and 45%, because of normal fluctuations in women's cycles. Very few women have a 28-day cycle every month.

- **Basal body temperature** (BBT) is the lowest body temperature when the body is at rest. When a woman ovulates, the rise in progesterone causes a corresponding rise in BBT. By charting her BBT, a woman can know when she *has* ovulated, but not when she *will* ovulate. Therefore, the method requires abstinence from the day the menstrual period stops until three or four days after the BBT increases. In about 20% of cycles, no rise in BBT registers, so the entire cycle must be considered unsafe.

  Success rates vary, but because the method is subject to so much error in recording and interpretation, it is generally considered unreliable as a contraceptive method. However, charting BBT is more effective when used to increase the likelihood of pregnancy.

- The **cervical mucus method,** also known as the *ovulation* or *Billings* method, or natural family planning, relies on detecting changes in a woman's cervical mucus around the time of ovulation.

For a few days before and a few days after menstruation, cervical discharge is absent. These days are considered safe for intercourse. Following this period, the cervical discharge is cloudy, thick and sticky. Gradually, it becomes clear, watery and slippery, similar to egg white. This type of mucus, called the *peak symptom*, lasts for only one or two days.

Ovulation generally occurs 24 hours after the last peak symptom day. Then the mucus is again thick and sticky. A couple using this method must abstain from sexual intercourse every day in which there is vaginal wetness, including menstruation and days of mucus flow.

The overall failure rate for this method is 19% to 23%. Several factors contribute to this high failure rate. In some women, the vagina is constantly wet due to infection or discharge. Sexual arousal always causes vaginal moisture.

Withdrawal

Withdrawal, or *coitus interruptus*, is an ancient and widely used method of contraception. The man simply removes his penis from the woman's vagina before ejaculation.

This is a difficult method to use. Men cannot always withdraw in time. The Cowper's glands secretions, which appear well in advance of ejaculation, may contain stray sperm.

The theoretical failure rate of withdrawal is 7%, but the actual failure rate is 18%. Even so, withdrawal is still much more effective than using no method at all.

Surgical Methods

Currently, the most effective means of birth control, other than total abstinence, is surgical sterilization. These relatively simple operations cause infertility in either men or women. Although there is a possibility that the surgeries can be reversed, the outcome of reversals is doubtful. Sterilization should be considered a permanent method of contraception and used only by people who are sure that they have all the children they want.

Among American married couples, sterilization is the most widely used method of avoiding unwanted pregnancies; one partner has been sterilized in about a third of all married couples using contraception.

■ **Vasectomy** is a simple procedure in which the tubes that carry sperm from the testes, the *vas deferens*, are cut. The operation can be done in a doctor's office in 15 minutes. Under a local anesthetic, the physician makes two small incisions through the scrotum. The vas are tied in two places and the segment between is removed. The ends are closed with heat, or cauterized, so the tubes cannot grow back together. The testicles continue to produce sperm, but sperm accumulate in the epididymis, where they die and are reabsorbed.

Vasectomy has no effect on sexual function. Testosterone levels stay the same, and men continue to have erections and ejaculate as before. The only difference is that the semen does not contain sperm.

Vasectomy is the most effective contraceptive; its theoretical and actual failure rates are both 0.15%. The rare failures are due to unprotected intercourse in the time immediately after the procedure, before full sterility has been achieved.

Vasectomy is a simple and safe operation. Complications occur in less than 5% of men who undergo the procedure.

■ **Tubal ligation** is the common method of surgical sterilization for healthy women. *Hysterectomy*, removal of the uterus, or *ovariectomy*, removal of the ovaries, will cause sterility, but these operations are not usually done for this purpose.

Tubal ligation literally means tying the fallopian tubes to prevent the sperm from meeting the egg, thus the common perception of a woman "having her tubes tied." Actually the tubes are cut, clipped or cauterized, which increases the effectiveness of the procedure.

Outpatient procedures performed under local anesthesia are the most popular techniques. Generally, a tube called a laparoscope is inserted through a small incision in the upper vagina, the abdomen or directly through the navel. The laparoscope allows the physician to see the fallopian tubes, which are then cut and closed.

The surgery does not interfere with normal sexual functions. Eggs are still ovulated and reabsorbed by the body. The ovaries continue to produce normal levels of hormones, so the menstrual cycle is not interrupted. There is no physiological effect on sexual interest or ability.

Tubal ligations offer almost 100% effectiveness. The 0.5% failure rate is due almost exclusively to unknown pregnancy at the time of sterilization.

As with any surgery, there is a risk of complications with female sterilization. However, serious complications are very rare. About 5% of women experience bleeding or infection in the first few days after surgery. For roughly one in 20,000 women, these complications become so serious they result in serious illness, even death. However, these risks are similar to those for most abdominal surgeries.

Teens and Contraception: The Facts

- Just under half of American teenagers are having sexual intercourse.
- More than 1 million American teenagers become pregnant each year; half of these pregnancies occur in the teenager's first six months of sexual activity.
- Four hundred thousand American teenagers have abortions each year, accounting for more than one-third of all U.S. abortions.
- More than half of teenage females don't use contraceptives the first time they have intercourse; more than a quarter never use any contraceptive.

Why Don't Teens Use Contraception?

Ignorance
- lack knowledge about the menstrual cycle and when pregnancy is likely to occur
- think they don't have intercourse often enough or aren't old enough to get pregnant
- think they are too young to buy contraceptives
- think birth control is too expensive
- do not know how to use contraceptive methods properly

Fear
- are afraid their parents will find out
- think that contraceptives are dangerous
- are embarrassed to be examined
- are afraid to talk to their partners about birth control

Lack of Maturity
- never got around to it
- never thought about it
- didn't believe pregnancy could happen to them, only to others

Other Reasons
- don't expect to have sex
- think birth control is wrong
- want to get pregnant
- sex is forced on them

Sexuality

Contraceptive Methods

Method	What is it?	Chances of *not* getting pregnant*	Health concerns	Strong points	Weak points
Condoms	■ Fits over erect penis and catches sperm when the man ejaculates.	If used carefully, 98%. If used with foam, more than 99%.	■ None.	■ Easily available. ■ Easy to use, easy to carry. ■ Used only during sex. ■ Best protection against AIDS and other sexually transmitted diseases (STDs).	■ Must be put on during sex. ■ Some men say it reduces sexual feelings. ■ Condoms with spermicide may irritate vagina or penis.
Diaphragm	■ Small rubber cup fits inside vagina, over the opening (cervix) to the womb (uterus). Used with contraceptive cream or jelly that kills sperm. ■ Must be fitted by clinician.	If used carefully, 97%.	■ Few health problems. ■ More bladder infections for some women. ■ Very small chance of toxic shock syndrome.	■ Can be put in 2 hours before sex. ■ Used only when needed. ■ May help protect against AIDS and other STD.	■ Can be hard to insert. ■ Can be messy. ■ Cream or jelly may irritate vagina or penis. ■ Must be left in place 6–8 hours after sex.

*Effectiveness rates from *Contraceptive Technology 1990–1992*. New York: Irvington Publishers, Inc., 1990.

HEALTH FACTS

CONTRACEPTIVE METHODS

Method	What is it?	Chances of *not getting pregnant**	Health concerns	Strong points	Weak points
Fertility Awareness Method	■ Woman charts body temperature, vaginal mucus, periods, which show when she can get pregnant and when she can't. ■ Can use condom, foam, sponge or diaphragm during her fertile time. ■ Special classes needed to learn.	If done carefully, 80%–98%.	■ None.	■ Allows intercourse with birth control during fertile time. ■ Helpful when ready to become pregnant.	■ Temperature and vaginal mucus must be charted *every day.* ■ Use of foam, sponge or diaphragm may make it hard to see changes in mucus. ■ If periods aren't regular, may not be as effective. ■ No protection against AIDS and other STD.
Foam, Suppositories, Cream & Jelly	■ Made of chemicals that kill sperm. ■ Put into vagina before intercourse.	If used carefully, 95%–97%. If used with condoms—more than 99%.	■ None.	■ Can be purchased in drugstores. ■ Easy to use, easy to carry. ■ Used only when needed. ■ May help protect against AIDS and other STD.	■ Must be put in no more than 20 minutes before sex. ■ Can be messy. ■ May irritate vagina or penis.

*Effectiveness rates from *Contraceptive Technology 1990–1992.* New York: Irvington Publishers, Inc., 1990.

Sexuality

Contraceptive Methods

Method	What is it?	Chances of *not getting pregnant**	Health concerns	Strong points	Weak points
IUD	■ Small device put inside womb by a clinician. ■ Not sure how it works. May stop fertilized egg from implanting and growing in womb.	95%–98%.	■ Increased chance of pelvic inflammatory disease (PID). ■ Increased chance of tubal pregnancy. ■ These 2 problems may make it hard to ever get pregnant. ■ Can puncture womb.	■ Always in place. ■ Doesn't interfere with sexual intercourse.	■ May cause more bleeding and cramping during period or spot bleeding. ■ If a woman gets pregnant, IUD must be taken out. ■ Should not be used by women with multiple partners. ■ No protection against AIDS and other STD.
Natural Family Planning	■ Woman charts body temperature, vaginal mucus, periods, which show when she can get pregnant and when she can't. ■ No intercourse during her fertile time. ■ Special classes needed to learn.	If done carefully, 80%–98%.	■ None.	■ Acceptable to most religious beliefs. ■ Helpful when ready to become pregnant.	■ Temperature and vaginal mucus must be charted every day. ■ No sex during fertile time. ■ If periods aren't regular, may not be as effective. ■ No protection against AIDS and other STD.

*Effectiveness rates from *Contraceptive Technology 1990–1992.* New York: Irvington Publishers, Inc., 1990.

CONTRACEPTIVE METHODS

Method	What is it?	Chances of *not* getting pregnant*	Health concerns	Strong points	Weak points
Norplant	■ Tiny capsules of artificial hormones put under skin of arm by a clinician. ■ Capsules slowly release hormones into bloodstream. ■ Stops ovaries from releasing an egg each month. ■ Thickens mucus in cervix, so it's hard for sperm to enter the womb.	More than 99%.	■ Few serious problems for most women. ■ Should not be used by women with liver disease, heart disease, breast cancer or blood clots.	■ Can stay in for 5 years. ■ Can be removed anytime, then woman can become pregnant right away. ■ Always in place. ■ Doesn't interfere with sexual intercourse.	■ For first few months, may cause irregular periods or spot bleeding. ■ Beginning costs are high ($400–$650). ■ Minor surgery required to insert or remove capsules. ■ No protection against AIDS and other STD.
Pill	■ Pills made of artificial hormones. ■ Stops ovaries from releasing an egg each month. ■ Must be prescribed by a clinician.	If used carefully, more than 99%.	■ Few serious problems for young women. ■ Small chance of blood clots, heart attacks and strokes. ■ May cause high blood pressure.	■ Simple and easy to use. ■ Doesn't interfere with sexual intercourse. ■ Less bleeding and cramping during period. ■ Less chance of PID.	■ May cause weight changes, moodiness, spotting, more vaginal infections. ■ Must be taken every day. ■ Not recommended for women over 35. ■ No protection against AIDS and other STD.

*Effectiveness rates from *Contraceptive Technology 1990–1992*. New York: Irvington Publishers, Inc., 1990.

Sexuality

Contraceptive Methods

Method	What is it?	Chances of *not* getting pregnant*	Health concerns	Strong points	Weak points
Sponge	■ Small, soft sponge fits inside vagina over opening (cervix) to womb. ■ Contains chemicals that kill sperm. ■ Sponge blocks or absorbs sperm.	If used carefully, 92%–95%.	■ Very small chance of toxic shock syndrome. ■ Should not be used during menstruation. ■ May increase chance of vaginitis.	■ Can be purchased in drugstores. ■ Easy to use, easy to carry. ■ Can be inserted several hours before sex and left in up to 24 hours. ■ Used only when needed. ■ May help protect against AIDS and other STD.	■ Can be hard to remove—sponge can tear. ■ Can make intercourse dry. ■ May irritate vagina or penis. ■ May not be effective for women who have had children.
Sterilization	■ Operation that makes a person unable to have a baby. ■ Permanent. ■ Both men and women can be sterilized.	99.6%.	■ Safer for men than for women. ■ Small chance of infection or bleeding after surgery. ■ Tubal pregnancy could occur if operation doesn't work.	■ No other birth control will ever be needed. ■ No physical effect on sexual desire or ability.	■ *Permanent.* Cannot be reversed later. ■ No protection against AIDS and other STD.

*Effectiveness rates from *Contraceptive Technology 1990–1992.* New York: Irvington Publishers, Inc., 1990.

HEALTH FACTS

1-Minute Facts

■ Humans have long tried to devise ways to prevent pregnancy.

■ All contraceptive methods, except abstinence, have some side effects or potential risks.

■ Abstinence is the safest and most effective way to avoid pregnancy and reduce the risk of contracting sexually transmitted disease.

■ Barrier methods of contraception work by preventing the sperm from reaching the egg.

■ Hormonal contraceptives are artificial hormone derivatives that prevent ovulation.

■ Intrauterine devices are inserted into the uterus to prevent pregnancy.

■ Fertility awareness techniques, such as the rhythm method, rely on understanding the timing of a woman's menstrual cycle to prevent pregnancy.

■ Surgical sterilization is the most effective means of birth control other than total abstinence.

■ There are many reasons why adolescents don't use contraceptives, including ignorance, fear and lack of maturity.

PUBERTY AND ADOLESCENCE

MYTH: Adolescence is the same thing as puberty.

Fact: Adolescence is the period of transition from the behaviors and attitudes of childhood to the behaviors and attitudes of adulthood. Puberty is the biological period of sexual maturation.

Puberty is the period of biological maturation from childhood to adulthood. During puberty, the reproductive system matures and the *secondary sex characteristics*, the physical sex differences between adult males and females, appear. As these changes occur, other parts of the body also grow, and social, psychological and intellectual maturity increase.

The transition takes from one to six years. It begins for some girls at ages ten or eleven, but doesn't begin for others until 15 or 16. Boys tend to enter puberty a year or two later than girls do. There is a wide age range among humans for each developmental event.

Adolescence is the interim between puberty and the attainment of adult status. It is a socially defined period of psychosocial transition from the behavior and attitudes of childhood to the behavior, attitudes and responsibilities of adulthood. Adolescent developmental tasks include:

- becoming independent from parents
- building skills to interact with peers
- defining a personal moral and ethical code
- adjusting to a new body and body image
- accepting the consequences of personal actions
- coping with new sexual feelings

Physical Changes at Puberty

The changes at puberty are triggered by hormones produced by the testes or ovaries, the brain's *hypothalamus* and *anterior pituitary*, and the *adrenal glands*. These hormones flow through the bloodstream to their "target" organs. Hormone production is regulated by the nervous system.

The brain-hormone system is functioning before puberty, but circulating levels of hormones are too low to mature the body. Scientists think the hypothalamus acts like a thermostat that becomes less sensitive to these hormones as the child grows. In other words, the "thermostat" stays off during childhood because it thinks the "temperature" is just right, but over time it senses the body is "cold" and turns up the "heat." An individual's mounting hormone levels finally reach a threshold that induces the body to respond.

A variety of changes occur during this growth period. Physical changes that aren't related to the reproductive system include:

- growth spurt
- weight gain
- acne
- increased muscle strength

- changing body proportions
- increased heart and lung capacity
- improved physical performance

■ **Growth spurt:** Although children grow in height through-out childhood, they grow at an amazing rate during the pubertal growth spurt. Boys on average grow three to five inches during their peak growth year; girls add only slightly less to their stature. Girls start growing first and are usually taller than boys of the same age from about ages 11 to 14.

■ **Weight gain:** Because the bones, muscles and internal organs grow, children gain weight. Some of the weight gain is due to increases in *subcutaneous fat*, the fat under the skin that contributes to shaping body contours. Women average more subcutaneous fat in the pelvic region, the breasts, the upper back, and the backs of the upper arms than men. This gives the female body its rounder contours.

■ **Acne:** This troublesome skin condition appears during puberty as a result of *androgens* (male sex hormones). Both boys and girls are affected, but boys tend to develop acne more often and to a more severe degree. Using over-the-counter preparations and keeping the skin clean will usu-ally keep the problem under control, but sometimes severe acne will require a doctor's attention.

■ **Muscle strength:** This increases for both sexes, but is more pronounced in boys. The body actually produces more and bigger muscle cells.

■ **Body proportions:** The proportions of the body change, too. The feet begin to grow about four months before the lower legs, and the legs begin to grow about a year before the trunk. This disproportionate pattern makes some ado-lescents look gangling and clumsy.

HEALTH FACTS

As the face elongates, the nose and jaw become more prominent and the lips fuller. Facial changes become more noticeable in males as facial hair begins to grow and the hairline on the head recedes.

■ **Heart and lungs:** Like other muscles, the heart grows to double its prepuberty size, with proportional increases in blood volume. Lungs and respiratory capacity grow, too.

■ **Physical performance:** Overall body growth means adults of both sexes have a much greater tolerance for physical exertion. Males have a slight advantage in strength and heart and lung functions, but the differences in physical abilities between men and women largely result from training. When women exercise to the same extent as men, they are just as strong, with only small differences in physical performance.

Reproductive Changes at Puberty

Puberty causes the internal and external sex organs to grow and function in an adult manner. It also causes the development of secondary sex characteristics, including breast and hair growth, and voice changes.

Maturation in Girls

Breast budding, which occurs between ages eight and thirteen, is usually the first sign of puberty in girls. Gradually, the nipple and areola enlarge, and the breast becomes more prominent.

Breast growth is controlled by estrogen and heredity. It is normal for the two breasts to develop at different rates. For most women, the breasts eventually even out, but many adult women have breasts slightly different in size. Breast growth is usually complete between ages 13 and 19.

Sexuality

Pubic hair appears slightly after breast growth begins. It precedes hair growth under the arms and on the legs by about one year. At first, the hair is lightly colored and sparse, gradually becoming darker and more abundant, forming the triangular adult pattern by about age 18.

The sex organs themselves change markedly in puberty. The muscles of the uterus develop. The vagina lengthens, and its interior walls become thicker and furrowed. It begins to lubricate more often. The clitoris and labia enlarge and become more erotically sensitive.

The ovaries begin to mature and release eggs, which starts the menstrual cycle. It is normal for the first period, or *menarche*, to occur between 8 and 16 years of age, with an average age of 12 to 13 years. The first ovulation will usually occur within one year following menarche, although in some girls, ovulation may occur prior to the first period.

Maturation in Boys

Puberty tends to begin one to two years later in boys than in girls. Enlargement of the testes between ages 10 and 13 is the first sign. This growth occurs because of increasing levels of testosterone, which also stimulates growth of the penis, prostate, seminal vesicles and epididymis.

Boys experience their first ejaculation at about age 11 or 12, but mature sperm usually, but not always, take a few more years to appear. Ejaculation is not possible before puberty because the prostate and seminal vesicles have not yet been stimulated by hormones to function.

As the reproductive organs mature, boys begin to experience erections and *nocturnal emissions* ("wet dreams") in their sleep. The reproductive system usually completes the transformation to adult structure and function in roughly four or five years.

Pubic hair growth occurs between the ages of 12 and 16. About two years after pubic hair appears, hair begins to grow under the arms and on the face. Male body hair patterns begin to develop, and chest hair will continue to grow for the next ten years.

Late in puberty, boys' voices begin to deepen, due to enlargement of the larynx and thickening of the vocal cords in response to testosterone. Girls' voices deepen, too, but not to the degree seen in boys.

Early and Late Bloomers

Physical and emotional development occurs over a wide age range, and everyone ends up at the same place eventually. Throughout this time, however, most adolescents perceive themselves to be different from others. The difference can have positive or negative effects.

Boys who mature early tend to be more self-confident, relaxed and popular with peers than late-maturing boys. Early-maturing girls tend to feel conspicuous, due to their tallness or bigger breasts, while late-maturing girls are often outgoing, confident leaders. Certainly, these perceptions are affected by culture and gender role expectations.

Adolescent Sexuality

The biological factors of puberty affect sexuality. For example, the growth of the sexual organs and development of secondary sex characteristics force young people to view themselves and others as sexual beings. Surges in sex hormones cause increased sexual drive.

Puberty also causes psychological shifts in sexuality. As the body changes from that of a child to that of an adult, major changes in self-perception and body image take place.

Adolescents often experience conflicting feelings about their changing bodies. On the one hand, they feel pride in their emerging manhood or womanhood. On the other, they feel concern and confusion. They worry about the shape and size of their body parts.

Gradually, adolescents become aware that their bodies now attract new attention from adults and peers. Parents communicate their acceptance or anxiety in various ways, making their children more comfortable or more uneasy. Other adults may express sexual interest, which is at once flattering and frightening.

Even without overt sexual interest, teens become acutely aware that society often measures self-worth in terms of personal attractiveness. Teens understand the value placed on physical attractiveness, so they bathe, comb their hair, worry about pimples—all in the pursuit of a socially acceptable image.

Self-image can affect self-esteem regardless of an individual's level of attractiveness. Young persons with low self-esteem are likely to be anxious and disapprove of their bodies no matter what the adult world thinks or says.

Compared to childhood, sexual interests and sexual behaviors intensify during adolescence. Pubertal hormone changes may in part be responsible for an increase in sex drive.

Social expectations also exert a strong influence on adolescent sexuality whatever the level of physical maturity. For example, school dances provide an early opportunity for boys and girls at all points along the developmental scale to interact. If dating is expected by a certain age, all youth of that age tend to engage in the activity regardless of their developmental level.

Adolescent sexuality begins to focus on erotic self-discovery and the formation of erotic relationships with others. Through these explorations, adolescents complete their sexual identity and develop a sexual value system.

COMMITMENT

Commitment is a promise to nurture and sustain a relationship. It usually implies exclusivity. Young couples experiment with various levels of commitment.
Some promise not to date other people, a private promise indicating this will be their only sexual relationship. The serial monogamy characteristic of many adolescent relationships can be considered a transient form of commitment.

1-Minute Facts

- Puberty is the period of biological maturation from childhood to adulthood, during which the reproductive system matures and the secondary sex characteristics appear.

- Adolescence is the socially defined period of transition that occurs between puberty and the attainment of adult status.

- Changes at puberty are triggered by hormones.

- Physical changes at puberty include growth spurt, weight gain, increased muscle strength, changing body proportions, increased heart and lung capacity, improved physical performance, and acne.

- Puberty causes the internal and external sex organs to grow and develop, and also causes the development of secondary sex characteristics.

- Puberty tends to begin one to two years later in boys than in girls.

- Physical and emotional development occurs over a wide age range.

- Both biological and psychological changes in puberty affect sexuality.

- Sexual interest and behaviors intensify during adolescence.

- Adolescent sexuality begins to focus on both erotic self-discovery and the formation of erotic relationships with others.

Love, Intimacy and Sexual Choices

Myth: Sexual desire is a sure sign of love.

Fact: Feeling attracted to someone does not mean one is in love with that person. Adolescents often confuse feelings of love and desire.

The relationship between love and sex is very complicated. They can exist apart from each other or together. They both can be passionate and consuming.

Love means different things to different people in different relationships at different times in their lives. At its most basic level, love is a state in which one person's happiness is essential to another's.

According to psychologist Robert Sternberg, love has three components: intimacy, passion and commitment.

- **Intimacy** is the feeling of warmth and connectedness in a relationship that comes from communicating openly and honestly, understanding each other and showing mutual respect.
- **Passion** includes drives that lead to romance, physical attraction and sexual interaction but can also include other strong needs—for example, attachment, self-esteem or dominance.
- **Commitment** is first the short-term decision that one person does, in fact, love another; then it becomes the long-term promise to nurture and sustain the relationship through all the inevitable ups and downs to come.

BUILDING INTIMACY

What makes a relationship intimate?
- **Cooperation:** Working together toward a common goal.
- **Communication:** Expressing affection and appreciation; listening and talking; resolving conflicts.
- **Self-disclosure:** Revealing private thoughts and feelings without fear of ridicule or rejection.
- **Caring:** Putting someone else's needs ahead of one's own without loss of identity.
- **Trust:** Having confidence in each other's honesty.

Sexuality

Stages of Romantic or Erotic Love

The following stages have been identified as aspects of romantic love:

- falling in love
- transitional love
- companionate love

■ **Falling in love:** This first stage is filled with powerful emotions. Psychologist Dorothy Tennov (1979) has termed this feeling *limerence*. Limerence is marked by preoccupation with thoughts of the loved one and the certain knowledge that only this one person can satisfy one's needs. Limerence is almost completely outside rational control. Its ups and downs can interfere with work, other relationships, even sleep and appetite.

■ **Transitional love:** Transition, or change, occurs in every relationship over time. In romantic love, the excitement of getting to know someone (intimacy) and the passion of a new sexual relationship decline. Lovers begin to notice imperfections in each other. Boredom or frustration can occur when the reality does not match fantasy.

This love stage is basically a time for testing reality—to confront the conflicts and doubts and to make a decision about the future of the relationship. If the conflicts can't be resolved, the partnership gradually dissolves.

■ **Companionate love:** No one can live indefinitely in the throes of limerence. Companionate love is the transformation of limerence into love that can meet the demands of adult life.

This type of love is most common among adults in long-term relationships such as marriage. It allows couples to work, raise children, serve the community and love each other in long-lasting, committed relationships.

Human Sexual Response

Human sexual response consists of a series of biological and psychological changes. Dr. William H. Masters and his colleague Virginia E. Johnson have divided human sexual response into the following four stages:

- excitement
- plateau
- orgasm
- resolution

■ **Excitement,** the first stage, can be stimulated by physical or psychological factors. During this phase, the male penis becomes erect and the female vagina begins to lubricate.

■ During **plateau,** the second stage, changes that began during the first phase continue. Some people consider this the highest stage of sexual arousal.

- **Orgasm** is the third stage. It involves both physical effects, contractions of the genitals, and a psychological change. In males, orgasm usually results in ejaculation. In females, it results in a series of pelvic muscle contractions.

- During **resolution,** the fourth stage of the cycle, the events of the first three stages are reversed.

Forms of Sexual Expression

There are many ways to express love and sexual feelings. Sexual intercourse is only one of those ways.

Possible choices include:
- abstinence
- masturbation
- dreams and fantasies
- touching
- sexual intercourse

- **Abstinence:** Choosing not to have intercourse is the safest and most effective way to avoid pregnancy and reduce the risk of sexually transmitted disease. It is free, requires no prescription or exam, is always available, is accepted religiously and morally, is reversible and has no side effects.

  Human beings practice abstinence for long periods in their lives, for example, during childhood and, for a great number of people, during adolescence. Adults make the choice to be abstinent as well.

  Abstinence does not mean people aren't sexual. They may engage in other forms of sexual expression, even to orgasm.

■ **Masturbation:** Although most children have stimulated their genitals prior to puberty, the rapid growth of the sex organs tends to be accompanied by an increase in the frequency of masturbation. Unlike young children, adolescents do have erotic intent when they masturbate.

Masturbation is the most common source of orgasm for both boys and girls in adolescence. About three-quarters of all teenagers have reached orgasm through self-stimulation.

Even though many young people and adults masturbate, guilt, anxiety and religious taboos continue to be associated with the practice. However, masturbation provides a safe sexual outlet for adolescents, through which they can learn about their own sexual responses and rehearse for adult sexual encounters. Masturbation offers a safe alternative to sexual intercourse for both youth and adults, because it presents no danger of pregnancy or sexually transmitted disease.

■ **Dreams and fantasies:** Dreams are fantasies that occur during sleep, and erotic dreams are quite common among all men and women. Adolescents typically have a rich fantasy life. Boys' sexual dreams may lead to nocturnal emissions, which are a visible sign orgasm has occurred. Girls do not ejaculate, but they are just as likely to have sexual dreams that lead to orgasm.

Besides providing sexual arousal, fantasies can add pleasure to other sexual activities such as masturbation or substitute for an unattainable experience. They provide a form of mental rehearsal for future experiences and a safe, controlled, unembarrassing means of sexual experimentation.

- **Touching:** Touching refers to activities that induce the sexual response but do not include intercourse. Touching can include kissing, hugging, caressing, and breast and genital stimulation with another person.

  The activities of touching are, in fact, identical to those of foreplay in preparation for sexual intercourse. However, touching can be seen as a satisfying sexual activity on its own, which does not need to lead to orgasm or intercourse. Touching activities range from less intense, such as holding hands, to more intense, such as mutual masturbation.

- **Sexual intercourse:** Touching usually precedes intercourse. There are three types of sexual intercourse: vaginal, oral and anal. Vaginal intercourse carries the possible consequence of pregnancy as well as sexually transmitted disease (STD).

  Oral intercourse may be used as a substitute for vaginal intercourse as a way to avoid pregnancy. However, it does not avoid the possibility of transmitting STD, including HIV infection.

  Anal intercourse also avoids the possibility of pregnancy, but unprotected anal sex carries a real possibility of disease. Condoms are also more likely to fail during anal sex.

Sexual Orientation

Gender identity is the personal, internal sense of oneself as male or female. Sexual orientation has to do with which gender arouses sexual feelings in an individual. Individuals who feel sexual attraction toward persons of the opposite sex are called *heterosexuals*; individuals who are attracted to persons of the same sex are called *homosexuals*. Some individuals are attracted to both sexes and are called *bisexuals*.

Kinsey and his colleagues illustrated sexual orientation on a seven-point continuum, reflecting the fact that no clear-cut line separates homosexuality and heterosexuality. The scale extends from 0, exclusive heterosexuality, to 6, exclusive homosexuality.

They also proposed that acts and stimuli, not people, be characterized as heterosexual or homosexual. Homosexual acts occur throughout most human culture, but homosexual orientations are less common than homosexual acts or heterosexual orientations.

Many myths and prejudices surround the topic of sexual orientation. One of the most pronounced prejudices is *homophobia,* learned fear and hatred toward homosexuals. Some people have trouble viewing homosexuals as individuals with rights and emotions. Strong homophobic feelings are often linked to myths that obscure the facts.

Homosexual contacts with peers in adolescence are quite common. Estimates for adolescents who have had at least one same-gender sexual experience range from 10% to 20%. These encounters are usually the result of curiosity.

Most young people who play same-sex erotic games do not consider themselves homosexual and do not necessarily go on to homosexuality in adulthood. Even though most adult homosexuals do recall that their first same-sex erotic behavior occurred in adolescence, a person who does not already have an emerging homosexual orientation prior to adolescence is unlikely to develop one.

1-Minute Facts

- The relationship between love and sex is very complicated.

- Stages of romantic love include falling in love, transitional love and companionate love.

- Human sexual response can be divided into four stages—excitement, plateau, orgasm and resolution.

- There are many forms of sexual expression.

- Sexual orientation indicates which gender arouses sexual feelings in an individual.

Glossary

A

abortion—Ending a pregnancy before a fetus could survive outside the uterus.

abstinence—Voluntarily not engaging in sexual intercourse.

Adam principle—Refers to the process of sexual differentiation by which something must be added to the system to force the process in a male direction; e.g., androgen hormones must be added during fetal development to form the male sexual organs instead of the female.

adolescence—The period between sexual maturity at puberty and the attainment of adult social status; psychosocial development during the teenage years.

adrenal glands—A pair of endocrine glands, located above the kidneys, that produce and secrete hormones, including androgens.

amenorrhea—The absence of menstruation.

amniotic fluid—The fluid within the amniotic sac that surrounds and protects the fetus.

androgens—Hormones that are primarily responsible for the development and maintenance of the male reproductive system, e.g., testosterone.

areola—The circular, darkened area of the breast surrounding the nipple.

autosomes—The 22 pairs of chromosomes that are the same in males and females.

B

basal body temperature—The temperature of the body at rest.

blastocyst—A small mass of cells with a fluid-filled hollow center produced after the fertilized egg has been dividing for a few days; attaches to the uterine lining at implantation.

C

cervix—The lower portion of the uterus, which projects into the vagina.

chromosome—The genetic material found in the nucleus of every human cell.

cilia—Hair-like structures that line the fallopian tubes and propel the egg toward the uterus.

circumcision—Surgical removal of the foreskin of the penis.

clitoris—A small, highly sensitive female genital organ.

colostrum—A thin yellowish fluid secreted by the breasts; a precursor to breast milk.

contraception—Any method of preventing pregnancy; also called birth control or family planning.

corona—The sensitive ridge where the glans and shaft meet on the penis.

corpora cavernosa—Two parallel masses of erectile tissue, located in the shaft of the penis and clitoris, that become engorged with blood during sexual arousal.

corpus luteum—The part of the ovarian follicle that is left in the ovary after the egg is released; its primary function is to secrete progesterone.

corpus spongiosum—A column of spongy, erectile tissue in the penis that contains the urethra and becomes engorged with blood during sexual arousal.

D

douche—To rinse out the inside of the vagina with water or chemical solutions.

drive—A basic biological impulse or urge.

duct—A narrow tubular channel, such as the vas deferens in the male and fallopian tubes in the female.

dysmenorrhea—Painful menstruation.

E

ectopic pregnancy—Pregnancy in which the fertilized egg implants outside the uterus, as in the fallopian tube.

ejaculation—The expulsion of semen from the penis.

embryo—Stage in prenatal development between the ovum and the fetus; stage of development between the second and eighth weeks of pregnancy.

endometrium—The inner lining of the uterus, which is partially shed during menstruation.

endometriosis—The growth of endometrial tissue outside the uterus.

estrogen—Hormone produced by the ovaries, responsible for female sexual maturation, regulation of the menstrual cycle, and maintenance of the vagina and uterine lining.

F

fallopian tubes—Two tubes that extend from the ovaries to the uterus.

fertilization—The union of the egg and sperm.

fetus—The latter stages of development from the ninth week of pregnancy to birth.

fimbriae—Fringed ends of the fallopian tubes nearest the ovaries.

follicle—A thin capsule of tissue surrounding an ovum.

follicle-stimulating hormone—The pituitary hormone, known as FSH, that stimulates maturation of ovarian follicles in the female and sperm production in the male.

foreplay—Kissing, touching, genital stimulation and other forms of physical contact between two people that lead to intercourse.

foreskin—The loose, movable fold of skin that covers the end of the penis; also called *prepuce*.

G

gamete—Sperm or egg cell.

gender identity—The personal, internal sense of oneself as male or female.

gender role—The behaviors, strongly influenced by culture, that indicate to oneself and others whether a person is male or female; the public expression of gender identity.

genitals—The male and female sex organs.

glans—The tip of the penis or clitoris; sometimes called head.

gonads—The testes or ovaries.

gonadotropins—Pituitary hormones that stimulate the ovaries or testes to secrete their own hormones.

gynecologist—A medical doctor who specializes in female anatomy and reproductive functions.

H

homophobia—Irrational fear of and hostility toward homosexuals.

hormones—Chemicals secreted by the endocrine glands, which affect function and behavior.

human chorionic gonadotropin—Hormone, known as HCG, produced by the cells of the developing embryo; found only in the blood or urine of pregnant women.

hymen—Thin membrane partially covering the opening of the vagina.

hypothalamus—Part of the brain that has control over most endocrine pathways and regulates sexual function.

hysterectomy—Surgical removal of the uterus.

I

implantation—The attachment of the blastocyst to the inner wall of the uterus.

impotence—Inability to have or maintain an erection sufficient for sexual intercourse despite stimulation; also called erectile dysfunction.

infertility—Inability to conceive a child after one year of unprotected intercourse.

instinct—Inborn tendency to behave in characteristic ways.

intercourse—A type of sexual contact involving one of the following: (1) insertion of a man's penis into a woman's vagina (vaginal intercourse); (2) placement of the mouth on the genitals of another person (oral intercourse) or (3) insertion of a man's penis into the anus of another person (anal intercourse).

interstitial cells—Cells located between the seminiferous tubules in the testes that produce testosterone.

L

labor—The process of giving birth, involving uterine contractions, dilation of cervix, the baby's birth and expulsion of the placenta.

lactation—Production of breast milk in the female.

libido—Sexual drive or energy.

ligament—A muscular attachment to underlying bone.

limerence—Term coined by Dorothy Tennov to describe being in love.

HEALTH FACTS

luteinizing hormone—A pituitary hormone, known as LH, that stimulates ovulation and the testes to produce androgens.

M

mammogram—A special breast X-ray used to detect cancer.

menarche—The first menstrual period.

menopause—Stage that marks the end of menstrual activity.

menstruation—Periodic discharge of a bloody fluid caused by the shedding of the uterine lining; occurs approximately once a month; also called menses or period.

mittelschmerz—Abdominal pain at the time of ovulation.

mons pubis—The soft, fatty tissue over the female pubic bone that becomes covered with hair after puberty; also called mons veneris.

morula—Round mass of cells developing from the zygote within a few days of fertilization.

motility—The ability of mature sperm to swim on their own.

myometrium—Muscular, middle layer of tissue in the uterus.

N

nocturnal emission—Involuntary discharge of semen during sleep; also called wet dream.

O

orgasm—Climactic, satisfying response to sexual stimulation, marking the sudden discharge of accumulated sexual tension.

P

Pap test—A routine test for cervical cancer in which a few cells are scraped from the cervix and examined.

perimetrium—The outer covering of the uterus.

phimosis—Condition in which the foreskin of the penis is so tight it cannot be pulled back over the glans.

pituitary gland—Small endocrine gland at the base of the brain that secretes hormones that turn on sexual development and functions.

placenta—The organ through which the fetus receives nutrients and oxygen from its mother and expels waste products.

progesterone—Hormone primarily produced by the corpus luteum that stimulates the development of the endometrium.

psychogenic—Made in the mind; can refer to erections that occur without physical stimulation of the penis.

puberty—Stage of life in which the reproductive system matures and secondary sex characteristics appear.

R

reflexogenic—Occurring as an involuntary response to a stimulus; can refer to erections that occur in response to any physical stimulation of the penis.

S

secondary sex characteristics—Physical signs, other than the genitals, that indicate sexual maturity, e.g., breasts, pubic hair, facial hair, deepened voice.

semen—Milky white fluid containing sperm, which is ejaculated from the penis.

sexual reproduction—Joining of a male and female gamete or sex cell to create a new organism.

shaft—The body of the penis or clitoris.

smegma—Yellowish substance composed of glandular secretions, dead cells, dirt particles and bacteria, which accumulate under the foreskin of the penis or the hood of the clitoris.

spermatogenesis—The development of sperm cells.

sphincter—Muscular ring that constricts body openings.

sterile—Incapable of reproducing.

synthetic—Not natural; produced in a laboratory by chemical reactions.

T

testosterone—Hormone mainly secreted by the testes in males and the adrenal glands in both sexes.

toxic shock syndrome—Illness, known as TSS, caused by the overgrowth of bacteria, associated with use of high absorbency tampons.

tubal ligation—Surgical procedure in which a woman is made sterile by cutting or tying the fallopian tubes.

U

umbilical cord—Cord that connects the fetus to the placenta.

V

vasectomy—Surgical procedure in which a man is made sterile by cutting or tying the vas deferens.

vulva—Collective term for the external female genitals; includes the mons pubis, the labia majora and minora, the clitoris, and the vaginal and urethral openings.

W

womb—The uterus.

Z

zygote—Single cell created by the union of egg and sperm.

Resources

American Association of Sex
  Educators, Counselors, and
  Therapists
Executive Director
435 North Michigan Ave.,
  Suite 1717
Chicago, IL 60611
312-644-0828

American Medical Association
Department of Health Education
515 N. State St.
Chicago, IL 60610
800-621-8335

American School Health
  Association
P.O. Box 708
Kent, OH 44240
216-678-1601

American Pharmaceutical
  Association
2215 Constitution Ave. NW
Washington, DC 20037
202-628-4410

Centers for Disease Control and
  Prevention (CDC)
Department of Adolescent and
  School Health
4770 Buford Highway NE
Atlanta, GA 30341
404-488-5323

Coalition on Sexuality and
  Disability
380 2nd Ave., 4th Floor
New York, NY 10010
212-242-3900

March of Dimes, Birth Defects
    Foundation
Public Health Education
    Department
1275 Mamaroneck Ave.
White Plains, NY 10605
914-428-7100

Masters and Johnson Institute
One Campbell Plaza
59th and Arsenal, Suite 4B
St. Louis, MO 63139
314-781-2224

National Clearinghouse for
    Maternal and Child Health
8201 Greensboro Dr., Suite 600
McLean, VA 22102
703-821-8955, ext. 254 or 265

National Gay and Lesbian
    Task Force
1734 14th St. NW
Washington, DC 20009
202-332-6483

Planned Parenthood Federation
    of America
810 Seventh Ave.
New York, NY 10019
212-541-7800

Sex Information and Education
    Council of the United States
    (SIECUS)
130 West 42nd St., Suite 2500
New York, NY 10036
212-819-9770

Sexuality

References

Allgeier, A., and E. Allgeier. 1988. *Sexual interactions. 2d ed.* Lexington, MA: D. C. Heath.

Bruess, C., and S. Laing. 1989. *Entering adulthood: Understanding reproduction, birth and contraception.* Santa Cruz, CA: ETR Associates.

Cassell, C. 1984. *Swept away: Why women fear their own sexuality.* New York: Simon and Schuster.

Crooks, R., and K. Baur. 1990. *Our sexuality. 4th ed.* Redwood City, CA: Benjamin/Cummings.

Freedman, D. 1992. The aggressive egg. *Discover* 13(6): 60–65.

Hubbard, B. M. 1989. *Entering adulthood: Living in relationships.* Santa Cruz, CA: ETR Associates.

Hyde, J. 1990. *Understanding human sexuality.* New York: McGraw-Hill.

Katchadourian, H. 1989. *Fundamentals of human sexuality. 5th ed.* Fort Worth, TX: Holt, Rinehart and Winston.

Kunz, J., ed. 1982. *The American Medical Association family medical guide.* New York: Random House.

Luria, Z., S. Friedman and M. D. Rose. 1987. *Human sexuality*. New York: John Wiley and Sons.

Masters, W., V. Johnson and R. Kolodny. 1992. *Human sexuality. 4th ed.* New York: HarperCollins.

McCary, S., and J. McCary. 1984. *Human sexuality. 3d ed.* Belmont, CA: Wadsworth.

Population Crisis Committee. 1985. *Issues in contraceptive development, No. 15.* Washington, DC.

Potts, M. 1992. Birth control. *Encyclopaedia Britannica.* Chicago, IL: Encyclopaedia Britannica.

Rice, F. P. 1989. *Human sexuality.* Dubuque, IA: Wm. C. Brown.

Tennov, D. 1979. *Love and limerence: The experience of being in love.* Chelsea, MI: Scarborough House.

Index

intercourse, 99, 107
IUDs (intrauterine devices),
   71–73, 81

labia majora, 7, 8–9
labia minora, 7, 9
labor, 51, 107
lactation, 107
LH (luteinizing hormone), 16–18,
   67, 108
libido, 107
ligament, 15, 107
limerence, 95, 107
love, 93–96

mammary glands, 10
mammogram, 22, 108
masturbation, 98
menarche, 16, 89, 108
menopause, 16, 68, 108
menstrual cycle, 13, 14, 15, 16–18
   problems with, 19–20
menstruation, 15, 108
mittelschmerz, 18, 108
mons pubis, 7, 8, 108
moral values, 2
morula, 46, 108
myometrium, 13, 108

nipple, 10–11, 88
nocturnal emissions and orgasms,
   21, 36, 89, 108

oral contraceptives, 54, 66–69, 82
oral intercourse, 107
ovarian cancer, 23
ovarian cysts, 23
ovaries, 12, 15
ovulation, 18, 89

Pap smears, 23, 61, 108
penis, 27–30
perimetrium, 13, 108
phimosis, 38, 109
pituitary gland, 16, 86, 109
placenta, 48, 109
PMS (premenstrual syndrome), 20
postcoital pills, 70–71
pregnancy, 43–50
prepuce. See foreskin
progesterone, 15, 16–18, 65, 109
progestins, 67
prostate cancer, 40
psychogenic erections, 35, 36, 109

puberty, 85, 86–90, 109

reflexogenic erections, 35, 109
rhythm methods, 73–75

scrotum, 28, 30
secondary sex characteristics, 85,
   88–90, 109
self-esteem, 91
semen, 36, 109
sexual orientation, 99–100
sexual reproduction, 43, 109
sexual response, 96–97
   female, 21
   male, 35–37
sexuality, ix–xi, 1–5
shaft, 9, 28, 109
smegma, 29, 109
smoking, 49
sperm, 14, 34–35, 40
spermatogenesis, 34, 109
spermicides, 57–58, 80
STD (sexually transmitted disease)
   protection, 58, 65
sterility, 14, 110
sterilization, 15, 54, 75–77, 83

tampons, 20
testicles, 30, 31–32
testicular cancer, 39
testicular self-examination, 39
testosterone, 32, 110
torsion, 38
TSS (toxic shock syndrome),
   20, 63, 110
tubal ligation, 15, 77, 110

umbilical cord, 48, 110
urethra, 10, 28, 33
uterine cancer, 23
uterus, 12, 13–14

vagina, 10, 12–13
vaginal intercourse, 107
vaginitis, 22, 58
values, 2–3
vasectomy, 32, 54, 76, 110
vulva, 7–10, 110

withdrawal, 75
womb, 13–14, 110

zygote, 46, 110

Sexuality